Also by E. H. C A R R

WHAT IS HISTORY?

"I often think it odd that it should be so dull, for a great deal of it must be invention."

Catherine Morland on History

(*Northanger Abbey*, Ch. XIV)

WHAT IS HISTORY?

The George Macaulay Trevelyan Lectures
Delivered in the University of Cambridge
January–March 1961

by

EDWARD HALLETT CARR

Fellow of Trinity College

New York · Alfred A. Knopf
1963

L. C. catalog card number: 61–17812

THIS IS A BORZOI BOOK,
PUBLISHED BY ALFRED A. KNOPF, INC.

Published January 22, 1962
Reprinted two times
Fourth printing, March 1963

A portion of the last chapter appeared in *The New Republic*.

CONTENTS

WHAT IS HISTORY?

CHAPTER I

THE HISTORIAN AND
HIS FACTS

WHAT is history? Lest anyone think the question
meaningless or superfluous, I will take as my text two
passages relating respectively to the first and second in-
carnations of *The Cambridge Modern History*. Here
is Acton in his report of October 1896 to the Syndics
of the Cambridge University Press on the work which
he had undertaken to edit:

It is a unique opportunity of recording, in the way most
useful to the greatest number, the fullness of the knowledge which the nineteenth century is about to bequeath.
. . . By the judicious division of labour we should be able
to do it, and to bring home to every man the last document, and the ripest conclusions of international research.
Ultimate history we cannot have in this generation; but
we can dispose of conventional history, and show the
point we have reached on the road from one to the other,
now that all information is within reach, and every problem has become capable of solution.[1]

And almost exactly sixty years later Professor Sir
George Clark, in his general introduction to the second *Cambridge Modern History*, commented on this

---

[1] *The Cambridge Modern History: Its Origin, Authorship and
Production* (Cambridge University Press; 1907), pp. 10–12.

belief of Acton and his collaborators that it would one day be possible to produce "ultimate history," and went on:

> Historians of a later generation do not look forward to any such prospect. They expect their work to be superseded again and again. They consider that knowledge of the past has come down through one or more human minds, has been "processed" by them, and therefore cannot consist of elemental and impersonal atoms which nothing can alter. . . . The exploration seems to be endless, and some impatient scholars take refuge in scepticism, or at least in the doctrine that, since all historical judgments involve persons and points of view, one is as good as another and there is no "objective" historical truth.[2] *eg. legend*

Where the pundits contradict each other so flagrantly the field is open to enquiry. I hope that I am sufficiently up-to-date to recognize that anything written in the 1890's must be nonsense. But I am not yet advanced enough to be committed to the view that anything written in the 1950's necessarily makes sense. Indeed, it may already have occurred to you that this enquiry is liable to stray into something even broader than the nature of history. The clash between Acton and Sir George Clark is a reflection of the change in our total outlook on society over the interval between these two pronouncements. Acton speaks out of the positive belief, the clear-eyed self-confidence of the later Victorian age; Sir George Clark echoes the be-

---

[2] *The New Cambridge Modern History*, I (Cambridge University Press; 1957), pp. xxiv-xxv.

wilderment and distracted scepticism of the beat generation. When we attempt to answer the question,
What is history?, our answer, consciously or unconsciously, reflects our own position in time, and forms
part of our answer to the broader question, what view
we take of the society in which we live. I have no fear
that my subject may, on closer inspection, seem trivial.
I am afraid only that I may seem presumptuous to
have broached a question so vast and so important.

The nineteenth century was a great age for facts.
"What I want," said Mr. Gradgrind in *Hard Times*,
"is Facts. . . . Facts alone are wanted in life." Nineteenth-century historians on the whole agreed with
him. When Ranke in the 1830's, in legitimate protest
against moralizing history, remarked that the task of
the historian was "simply to show how it really was
(*wie es eigentlich gewesen*)" this not very profound
aphorism had an astonishing success. Three generations of German, British, and even French historians
marched into battle intoning the magic words, "*Wie
es eigentlich gewesen*" like an incantation—designed,
like most incantations, to save them from the tiresome obligation to think for themselves. The Positivists, anxious to stake out their claim for history as
a science, contributed the weight of their influence to
this cult of facts. First ascertain the facts, said the
positivists, then draw your conclusions from them. In
Great Britain, this view of history fitted in perfectly

with the empiricist tradition which was the dominant strain in British philosophy from Locke to Bertrand Russell. The empirical theory of knowledge presupposes a complete separation between subject and object. Facts, like sense-impressions, impinge on the observer from outside, and are independent of his consciousness. The process of reception is passive: having received the data, he then acts on them. *The Shorter Oxford English Dictionary*, a useful but tendentious work of the empirical school, clearly marks the separateness of the two processes by defining a fact as "a datum of experience as distinct from conclusions." This is what may be called the common-sense view of history. History consists of a corpus of ascertained facts. The facts are available to the historian in documents, inscriptions, and so on, like fish on the fishmonger's slab. The historian collects them, takes them home, and cooks and serves them in whatever style appeals to him. Acton, whose culinary tastes were austere, wanted them served plain. In his letter of instructions to contributors to the first *Cambridge Modern History* he announced the requirement "that our Waterloo must be one that satisfies French and English, German and Dutch alike; that nobody can tell, without examining the list of authors where the Bishop of Oxford laid down the pen, and whether Fairbairn or Gasquet, Liebermann or Harrison took it up." [8] Even Sir George Clark, critical as he was of Acton's

---

[8] Acton: *Lectures on Modern History* (London: Macmillan & Co.; 1906), p. 318.

attitude, himself contrasted the "hard core of facts" in history with the "surrounding pulp of disputable interpretation" [4]—forgetting perhaps that the pulpy part of the fruit is more rewarding than the hard core. First get your facts straight, then plunge at your peril into the shifting sands of interpretation—that is the ultimate wisdom of the empirical, common-sense school of history. It recalls the favourite dictum of the great liberal journalist C. P. Scott: "Facts are sacred, opinion is free."

Now this clearly will not do. I shall not embark on a philosophical discussion of the nature of our knowledge of the past. Let us assume for present purposes that the fact that Caesar crossed the Rubicon and the fact that there is a table in the middle of the room are facts of the same or of a comparable order, that both these facts enter our consciousness in the same or in a comparable manner, and that both have the same objective character in relation to the person who knows them. But, even on this bold and not very plausible assumption, our argument at once runs into the difficulty that not all facts about the past are historical facts, or are treated as such by the historian. What is the criterion which distinguishes the facts of history from other facts about the past?

What is a historical fact? This is a crucial question into which we must look a little more closely. According to the common-sense view, there are certain basic

---

facts which are the same for all historians and which form, so to speak, the backbone of history—the fact, for example, that the Battle of Hastings was fought in 1066. But this view calls for two observations. In the first place, it is not with facts like these that the historian is primarily concerned. It is no doubt important to know that the great battle was fought in 1066 and not in 1065 or 1067, and that it was fought at Hastings and not at Eastbourne or Brighton. The historian must not get these things wrong. But when points of this kind are raised, I am reminded of Housman's remark that "accuracy is a duty, not a virtue." [5] To praise a historian for his accuracy is like praising an architect for using well-seasoned timber or properly mixed concrete in his building. It is a necessary condition of his work, but not his essential function. It is precisely for matters of this kind that the historian is entitled to rely on what have been called the "auxiliary sciences" of history—archaeology, epigraphy, numismatics, chronology, and so forth. The historian is not required to have the special skills which enable the expert to determine the origin and period of a fragment of pottery or marble, to decipher an obscure inscription, or to make the elaborate astronomical calculations necessary to establish a precise date. These so-called basic facts which are the same for all historians commonly belong to the category of the raw materials of the historian rather than of history itself.

---

[5] M. Manilius: *Astronomicon: Liber Primus,* 2nd. ed. (Cambridge University Press; 1937), p. 87.

The second observation is that the necessity to establish these basic facts rests not on any quality in the facts themselves, but on an *a priori* decision of the historian. In spite of C. P. Scott's motto, every journalist knows today that the most effective way to influence opinion is by the selection and arrangement of the appropriate facts. It used to be said that facts speak for themselves. This is, of course, untrue. The facts speak only when the historian calls on them: it is he who decides to which facts to give the floor, and in what order or context. It was, I think, one of Pirandello's characters who said that a fact is like a sack—it won't stand up till you've put something in it. The only reason why we are interested to know that the battle was fought at Hastings in 1066 is that historians regard it as a major historical event. It is the historian who has decided for his own reasons that Caesar's crossing of that petty stream, the Rubicon, is a fact of history, whereas the crossing of the Rubicon by millions of other people before or since interests nobody at all. The fact that you arrived in this building half an hour ago on foot, or on a bicycle, or in a car, is just as much a fact about the past as the fact that Caesar crossed the Rubicon. But it will probably be ignored by historians. Professor Talcott Parsons once called science "a selective system of cognitive orientations to reality." [6] It might perhaps have been put

---

[6] Talcott Parsons and Edward A. Shils: *Toward a General Theory of Action*, 3rd. ed. (Cambridge, Mass.: Harvard University Press; 1954), p. 167.

more simply. But history is, among other things, that.
The historian is necessarily selective. The belief in a
hard core of historical facts existing objectively and
independently of the interpretation of the historian
is a preposterous fallacy, but one which it is very hard
to eradicate.

Let us take a look at the process by which a mere
fact about the past is transformed into a fact of history. At Stalybridge Wakes in 1850, a vendor of gin-
gerbread, as the result of some petty dispute, was deliberately kicked to death by an angry mob. Is this a
fact of history? A year ago I should unhesitatingly
have said "no." It was recorded by an eyewitness in
some little-known memoirs;[7] but I had never seen it
judged worthy of mention by any historian. A year
ago Dr. Kitson Clark cited it in his Ford lectures in
Oxford.[8] Does this make it into a historical fact? Not,
I think, yet. Its present status, I suggest, is that it has
been proposed for membership of the select club of
historical facts. It now awaits a seconder and sponsors.
It may be that in the course of the next few years we
shall see this fact appearing first in footnotes, then in
the text, of articles and books about nineteenth-
century England, and that in twenty or thirty years'
time it may be a well established historical fact. Al-
ternatively, nobody may take it up, in which case it

---

[7] Lord George Sanger: *Seventy Years a Showman* (London:
J. M. Dent & Sons; 1926); pp. 188–9.

[8] These will shortly be published under the title *The Making of
Victorian England*.

will relapse into the limbo of unhistorical facts about the past from which Dr. Kitson Clark has gallantly attempted to rescue it. What will decide which of these two things will happen? It will depend, I think, on whether the thesis or interpretation in support of which Dr. Kitson Clark cited this incident is accepted by other historians as valid and significant. Its status as a historical fact will turn on a question of interpretation. This element of interpretation enters into every fact of history.

May I be allowed a personal reminiscence? When I studied ancient history in this university many years ago, I had as a special subject "Greece in the period of the Persian Wars." I collected fifteen or twenty volumes on my shelves and took it for granted that there, recorded in these volumes, I had all the facts relating to my subject. Let us assume—it was very nearly true —that those volumes contained all the facts about it that were then known, or could be known. It never occurred to me to enquire by what accident or process of attrition that minute selection of facts, out of all the myriad facts that must have once been known to somebody, had survived to become *the* facts of history. I suspect that even today one of the fascinations of ancient and mediaeval history is that it gives us the illusion of having all the facts at our disposal within a manageable compass: the nagging distinction between the facts of history and other facts about the past vanishes because the few known facts are all facts of history. As Bury, who had worked in both periods,

said, "the records of ancient and mediaeval history are
starred with lacunae." [9] History has been called an
enormous jig-saw with a lot of missing parts. But the
main trouble does not consist of the lacunae. Our
picture of Greece in the fifth century B.C. is defective
not primarily because so many of the bits have been
accidentally lost, but because it is, by and large, the
picture formed by a tiny group of people in the city
of Athens. We know a lot about what fifth-century
Greece looked like to an Athenian citizen; but hardly
anything about what it looked like to a Spartan, a
Corinthian, or a Theban—not to mention a Persian,
or a slave or other non-citizen resident in Athens. Our
picture has been pre-selected and predetermined for
us, not so much by accident as by people who were
consciously or unconsciously imbued with a particular
view and thought the facts which supported that view
worth preserving. In the same way, when I read in a
modern history of the Middle Ages that the people of
the Middle Ages were deeply concerned with religion,
I wonder how we know this, and whether it is true.
What we know as the facts of mediaeval history have
almost all been selected for us by generations of
chroniclers who were professionally occupied in the
theory and practice of religion, and who therefore
thought it supremely important, and recorded everything relating to it, and not much else. The picture
of the Russian peasant as devoutly religious was de-

---

[9] John Bagnell Bury: *Selected Essays* (Cambridge University
Press; 1930), p. 52.

stroyed by the revolution of 1917. The picture of mediaeval man as devoutly religious, whether true or not,
is indestructible, because nearly all the known facts
about him were pre-selected for us by people who believed it, and wanted others to believe it, and a mass
of other facts, in which we might possibly have found
evidence to the contrary, has been lost beyond recall.
The dead hand of vanished generations of historians,
scribes, and chroniclers has determined beyond the
possibility of appeal the pattern of the past. "The
history we read," writes Professor Barraclough, himself trained as a mediaevalist, "though based on facts,
is, strictly speaking, not factual at all, but a series of
accepted judgments." [1]

But let us turn to the different, but equally grave,
plight of the modern historian. The ancient or mediaeval historian may be grateful for the vast winnowing
process which, over the years, has put at his disposal
a manageable corpus of historical facts. As Lytton
Strachey said in his mischievous way, "ignorance is
the first requisite of the historian, ignorance which
simplifies and clarifies, which selects and omits." [2]
When I am tempted, as I sometimes am, to envy the
extreme competence of colleagues engaged in writing
ancient or mediaeval history, I find consolation in the
reflexion that they are so competent mainly because
they are so ignorant of their subject. The modern his-

---

[1] Geoffrey Barraclough: *History in a Changing World* (London:
Basil Blackwell & Mott; 1955), p. 14.
[2] Lytton Strachey: Preface to *Eminent Victorians*.

torian enjoys none of the advantages of this built-in
ignorance. He must cultivate this necessary ignorance
for himself—the more so the nearer he comes to his
own times. He has the dual task of discovering the few
significant facts and turning them into facts of history, and of discarding the many insignificant facts as
unhistorical. But this is the very converse of the nineteenth-century heresy that history consists of the compilation of a maximum number of irrefutable and objective facts. Anyone who succumbs to this heresy will
either have to give up history as a bad job, and take
to stamp-collecting or some other form of antiquarian-
ism, or end in a madhouse. It is this heresy, which
during the past hundred years has had such devastat-
ing effects on the modern historian, producing in Germany, in Great Britain, and in the United States a
vast and growing mass of dry-as-dust factual histories,
of minutely specialized monographs, of would-be historians knowing more and more about less and less,
sunk without trace in an ocean of facts. It was, I suspect, this heresy—rather than the alleged conflict between liberal and Catholic loyalties—which frustrated
Acton as a historian. In an early essay he said of his
teacher Döllinger: "He would not write with imperfect materials, and to him the materials were always
imperfect." [3] Acton was surely here pronouncing an

---

[3] Quoted in George P. Gooch: *History and Historians in the
Nineteenth Century* (London: Longmans, Green & Company;
1952), p. 385. Later Acton said of Döllinger that "it was given him
to form his philosophy of history on the largest induction ever avail-

anticipatory verdict on himself, on that strange phenomenon of a historian whom many would regard as the most distinguished occupant the Regius Chair of Modern History in this university has ever had—but who wrote no history. And Acton wrote his own epitaph in the introductory note to the first volume of the *Cambridge Modern History*, published just after his death, when he lamented that the requirements pressing on the historian "threaten to turn him from a man of letters into the compiler of an encyclopedia."[4] Something had gone wrong. What had gone wrong was the belief in this untiring and unending accumulation of hard facts as the foundation of history, the belief that facts speak for themselves and that we cannot have too many facts, a belief at that time so unquestioning that few historians then thought it necessary—and some still think it unnecessary today—to ask themselves the question: What is history?

The nineteenth-century fetishism of facts was completed and justified by a fetishism of documents. The documents were the Ark of the Covenant in the temple of facts. The reverent historian approached them with bowed head and spoke of them in awed tones. If you find it in the documents, it is so. But what, when we get down to it, do these documents—the decrees, the treaties, the rent-rolls, the blue books, the official correspondence, the private letters and diaries

---

able to man" (*History of Freedom and Other Essays* [London: Macmillan & Co.; 1907], p. 435).

[4] *The Cambridge Modern History*, I (1902), p. 4.

—tell us? No document can tell us more than what the author of the document thought—what he thought had happened, what he thought ought to happen or would happen, or perhaps only what he wanted others to think he thought, or even only what he himself thought he thought. None of this means anything until the historian has got to work on it and deciphered it. The facts, whether found in documents or not, have still to be processed by the historian before he can make any use of them: the use he makes of them is, if I may put it that way, the processing process.

Let me illustrate what I am trying to say by an example which I happen to know well. When Gustav Stresemann, the Foreign Minister of the Weimar Republic, died in 1929, he left behind him an enormous mass—300 boxes full—of papers, official, semi-official, and private, nearly all relating to the six years of his tenure of office as Foreign Minister. His friends and relatives naturally thought that a monument should be raised to the memory of so great a man. His faithful secretary Bernhardt got to work; and within three years there appeared three massive volumes, of some 600 pages each, of selected documents from the 300 boxes, with the impressive title *Stresemanns Vermächtnis*. In the ordinary way the documents themselves would have mouldered away in some cellar or attic and disappeared for ever; or perhaps in a hundred years or so some curious scholar would have come upon them and set out to compare them with Bernhardt's text. What happened was far more dramatic. In 1945 the documents fell into the hands of the British and the American governments, who photographed the lot and put the photostats at the disposal of scholars in the Public Record Office in London and in the National Archives in Washington, so that, if we have sufficient patience and curiosity, we can discover exactly what Bernhardt did. What he did was neither very unusual nor very shocking. When Stresemann died, his Western policy seemed to have been crowned with a series of brilliant successes—Locarno, the admission of Germany to the League of Nations, the Dawes and Young plans and the American loans, the withdrawal of allied occupation armies from the Rhineland. This seemed the important and rewarding part of Stresemann's foreign policy; and it was not unnatural that it should have been over-represented in Bernhardt's selection of documents. Stresemann's Eastern policy, on the other hand, his relations with the Soviet Union, seemed to have led nowhere in particular; and, since masses of documents about negotiations which yielded only trivial results were not very interesting and added nothing to Stresemann's reputation, the process of selection could be more rigorous. Stresemann in fact devoted a far more constant and anxious attention to relations with the Soviet Union, and they played a far larger part in his foreign policy as a whole, than the reader of the Bernhardt selection would surmise. But the Bernhardt volumes compare favorably, I suspect, with many published collections of documents on which the ordinary historian implicitly relies.

This is not the end of my story. Shortly after the publication of Bernhardt's volumes, Hitler came into power. Stresemann's name was consigned to oblivion in Germany, and the volumes disappeared from circulation: many, perhaps most, of the copies must have been destroyed. Today *Stresemanns Vermächtnis* is a rather rare book. But in the West Stresemann's reputation stood high. In 1935 an English publisher brought out an abbreviated translation of Bernhardt's work—a selection from Bernhardt's selection; perhaps one third of the original was omitted. Sutton, a well-known translator from the German, did his job competently and well. The English version, he explained in the preface, was "slightly condensed, but only by the omission of a certain amount of what, it was felt, was more ephemeral matter . . . of little interest to English readers or students." [5] This again is natural enough. But the result is that Stresemann's Eastern policy, already under-represented in Bernhardt, recedes still further from view, and the Soviet Union appears in Sutton's volumes merely as an occasional and rather unwelcome intruder in Stresemann's predominantly Western foreign policy. Yet it is safe to say that, for all except a few specialists, Sutton and not Bernhardt—and still less the documents themselves—

---

[5] *Gustav Stresemann: His Diaries, Letters, and Papers* (London: Macmillan & Co.; 1935), I, Editor's Note.

represents for the Western world the authentic voice of Stresemann. Had the documents perished in 1945 in the bombing, and had the remaining Bernhardt volumes disappeared, the authenticity and authority of Sutton would never have been questioned. Many printed collections of documents gratefully accepted by historians in default of the originals rest on no securer basis than this.

But I want to carry the story one step further. Let us forget about Bernhardt and Sutton, and be thankful that we can, if we choose, consult the authentic papers of a leading participant in some important events of recent European history. What do the papers tell us? Among other things they contain records of some hundreds of Stresemann's conversations with the Soviet ambassador in Berlin and of a score or so with Chicherin. These records have one feature in common. They depict Stresemann as having the lion's share of the conversations and reveal his arguments as invariably well put and cogent, while those of his partner are for the most part scanty, confused, and unconvincing. This is a familiar characteristic of all records of diplomatic conversations. The documents do not tell us what happened, but only what Stresemann thought had happened, or what he wanted others to think, or perhaps what he wanted himself to think, had happened. It was not Sutton or Bernhardt, but Stresemann himself, who started the process of selection. And, if we had, say, Chicherin's records of these same conversations, we should still learn from them only what Chicherin thought, and what really happened would still have to be reconstructed in the mind of the historian. Of course, facts and documents are essential to the historian. But do not make a fetish of them. They do not by themselves constitute history; they provide in themselves no ready-made answer to this tiresome question: What is history?

At this point I should like to say a few words on the question of why nineteenth-century historians were generally indifferent to the philosophy of history. The term was invented by Voltaire, and has since been used in different senses; but I shall take it to mean, if I use it at all, our answer to the question: What is history? The nineteenth century was, for the intellectuals of Western Europe, a comfortable period exuding confidence and optimism. The facts were on the whole satisfactory; and the inclination to ask and answer awkward questions about them was correspondingly weak. Ranke piously believed that divine providence would take care of the meaning of history if he took care of the facts; and Burckhardt with a more modern touch of cynicism observed that "we are not initiated into the purposes of the eternal wisdom." Professor Butterfield as late as 1931 noted with apparent satisfaction that "historians have reflected little upon the nature of things and even the nature of their own subject." [6] But my predecessor in these lectures, Dr. A. L.

---

[6] Herbert Butterfield: *The Whig Interpretation of History* (London: George Bell & Sons; 1931), p. 67.

Rowse, more justly critical, wrote of Sir Winston Churchill's *The World Crisis*—his book about the First World War—that, while it matched Trotsky's *History of the Russian Revolution* in personality, vividness, and vitality, it was inferior in one respect: it had "no philosophy of history behind it." [7] British historians refused to be drawn, not because they believed that history had no meaning, but because they believed that its meaning was implicit and self-evident. The liberal nineteenth-century view of history had a close affinity with the economic doctrine of *laissez-faire*—also the product of a serene and self-confident outlook on the world. Let everyone get on with his particular job, and the hidden hand would take care of the universal harmony. The facts of history were themselves a demonstration of the supreme fact of a beneficent and apparently infinite progress towards higher things. This was the age of innocence, and historians walked in the Garden of Eden, without a scrap of philosophy to cover them, naked and unashamed before the god of history. Since then, we have known Sin and experienced a Fall; and those historians who today pretend to dispense with a philosophy of history are merely trying, vainly and self-consciously, like members of a nudist colony, to recreate the Garden of Eden in their garden suburb. Today the awkward question can no longer be evaded.

· · ·

[7] Alfred L. Rowse: *The End of an Epoch* (London: Macmillan & Co.; 1947), pp. 282–3.

During the past fifty years a good deal of serious work has been done on the question: What is history? It was from Germany, the country which was to do so much to upset the comfortable reign of nineteenth-century liberalism, that the first challenge came in the 1880's and 1890's to the doctrine of the primacy and autonomy of facts in history. The philosophers who made the challenge are now little more than names: Dilthey is the only one of them who has recently received some belated recognition in Great Britain. Before the turn of the century, prosperity and confidence were still too great in this country for any attention to be paid to heretics who attacked the cult of facts. But early in the new century, the torch passed to Italy, where Croce began to propound a philosophy of history which obviously owed much to German masters. All history is "contemporary history," declared Croce,[8] meaning that history consists essentially in seeing the past through the eyes of the present and in the light of its problems, and that the main work of the historian is not to record, but to evaluate; for, if he does not evaluate, how can he know what is worth recording? In 1910 the American philosopher, Carl Becker, argued in deliberately provocative language that "the

---

[8] The context of this celebrated aphorism is as follows: "The practical requirements which underlie every historical judgment give to all history the character of 'contemporary history,' because, however remote in time events thus recounted may seem to be, the history in reality refers to present needs and present situations wherein those events vibrate" (Benedetto Croce: *History as the Story of Liberty* [London: George Allen & Unwin; 1941], p. 19).

facts of history do not exist for any historian till he creates them." [9] These challenges were for the moment little noticed. It was only after 1920 that Croce began to have a considerable vogue in France and Great Britain. This was not perhaps because Croce was a subtler thinker or a better stylist than his German predecessors, but because, after the First World War, the facts seemed to smile on us less propitiously than in the years before 1914, and we were therefore more accessible to a philosophy which sought to diminish their prestige. Croce was an important influence on the Oxford philosopher and historian Collingwood, the only British thinker in the present century who has made a serious contribution to the philosophy of history. He did not live to write the systematic treatise he had planned; but his published and unpublished papers on the subject were collected after his death in a volume entitled *The Idea of History*, which appeared in 1945.

The views of Collingwood can be summarized as follows. The philosophy of history is concerned neither with "the past by itself" nor with "the historian's thought about it by itself," but with "the two things in their mutual relations." (This dictum reflects the two current meanings of the word "history"—the enquiry conducted by the historian and the series of past events into which he enquires.) "The past which a historian studies is not a dead past, but a past which in some sense is still living in the present." But a past act is dead, *i.e.* meaningless to the historian, unless he can understand the thought that lay behind it. Hence "all history is the history of thought," and "history is the re-enactment in the historian's mind of the thought whose history he is studying." The reconstitution of the past in the historian's mind is dependent on empirical evidence. But it is not in itself an empirical process, and cannot consist in a mere recital of facts. On the contrary, the process of reconstitution governs the selection and interpretation of the facts: this, indeed, is what makes them historical facts. "History," says Professor Oakeshott, who on this point stands near to Collingwood, "is the historian's experience. It is 'made' by nobody save the historian: to write history is the only way of making it." [1]

This searching critique, though it may call for some serious reservations, brings to light certain neglected truths.

In the first place, the facts of history never come to us "pure," since they do not and cannot exist in a pure form: they are always refracted through the mind of the recorder. It follows that when we take up a work of history, our first concern should be not with the facts which it contains but with the historian who wrote it. Let me take as an example the great historian in whose honour and in whose name these lectures were founded. Trevelyan, as he tells us in his auto-

---

[1] Michael Oakeshott: *Experience and Its Modes* (Cambridge University Press; 1933), p. 99.

biography, was "brought up at home on a somewhat exuberantly Whig tradition"; [2] and he would not, I hope, disclaim the title if I described him as the last and not the least of the great English liberal historians of the Whig tradition. It is not for nothing that he traces back his family tree, through the great Whig historian George Otto Trevelyan, to Macaulay, incomparably the greatest of the Whig historians. Dr. Trevelyan's finest and maturest work *England under Queen Anne* was written against that background, and will yield its full meaning and significance to the reader only when read against that background. The author, indeed, leaves the reader with no excuse for failing to do so. For if, following the technique of connoisseurs of detective novels, you read the end first, you will find on the last few pages of the third volume the best summary known to me of what is nowadays called the Whig interpretation of history; and you will see that what Trevelyan is trying to do is to investigate the origin and development of the Whig tradition, and to roof it fairly and squarely in the years after the death of its founder, William III. Though this is not, perhaps, the only conceivable interpretation of the events of Queen Anne's reign, it is a valid and, in Trevelyan's hands, a fruitful interpretation. But, in order to appreciate it at its full value, you have to understand what the historian is doing. For if, as Collingwood says, the historian must re-enact in thought what

---

[2] G. M. Trevelyan: *An Autobiography* (London: Longmans, Green & Company; 1949), p. 11.

has gone on in the mind of his *dramatis personae,* so the reader in his turn must re-enact what goes on in the mind of the historian. Study the historian before you begin to study the facts. This is, after all, not very abstruse. It is what is already done by the intelligent undergraduate who, when recommended to read a work by that great scholar Jones of St. Jude's, goes round to a friend at St. Jude's to ask what sort of chap Jones is, and what bees he has in his bonnet. When you read a work of history, always listen out for the buzzing. If you can detect none, either you are tone deaf or your historian is a dull dog. The facts are really not at all like fish on the fishmonger's slab. They are like fish swimming about in a vast and sometimes inaccessible ocean; and what the historian catches will depend partly on chance, but mainly on what part of the ocean he chooses to fish in and what tackle he chooses to use—these two factors being, of course, determined by the kind of fish he wants to catch. By and large, the historian will get the kind of facts he wants. History means interpretation. Indeed, if, standing Sir George Clark on his head, I were to call history "a hard core of interpretation surrounded by a pulp of disputable facts," my statement would, no doubt, be one-sided and misleading, but no more so, I venture to think, than the original dictum.

The second point is the more familiar one of the historian's need of imaginative understanding for the minds of the people with whom he is dealing, for the thought behind their acts: I say "imaginative understanding," not "sympathy," lest sympathy should be supposed to imply agreement. The nineteenth century was weak in mediaeval history, because it was too much repelled by the superstitious beliefs of the Middle Ages and by the barbarities which they inspired, to have any imaginative understanding of mediaeval people. Or take Burckhardt's censorious remark about the Thirty Years' War: "It is scandalous for a creed, no matter whether it is Catholic or Protestant, to place its salvation above the integrity of the nation." [3] It was extremely difficult for a nineteenth-century liberal historian, brought up to believe that it is right and praiseworthy to kill in defence of one's country, but wicked and wrong-headed to kill in defence of one's religion, to enter into the state of mind of those who fought the Thirty Years' War. This difficulty is particularly acute in the field in which I am now working. Much of what has been written in English-speaking countries in the last ten years about the Soviet Union, and in the Soviet Union about the English-speaking countries, has been vitiated by this inability to achieve even the most elementary measure of imaginative understanding of what goes on in the mind of the other party, so that the words and actions of the other are always made to appear malign, senseless, or hypocritical. History cannot be written unless the historian can achieve some kind of contact with the mind of those about whom he is writing.

[3] Jacob Burckhardt: *Judgments on History and Historians* (London: S. J. Reginald Saunders & Company; 1958), p. 179.

3   The third point is that we can view the past, and achieve our understanding of the past, only through the eyes of the present. The historian is of his own age, and is bound to it by the conditions of human existence. The very words which he uses—words like democracy, empire, war, revolution—have current connotations from which he cannot divorce them. Ancient historians have taken to using words like *polis* and *plebs* in the original, just in order to show that they have not fallen into this trap. This does not help them. They, too, live in the present, and cannot cheat themselves into the past by using unfamiliar or obsolete words, any more than they would become better Greek or Roman historians if they delivered their lectures in a *chlamys* or a *toga*. The names by which successive French historians have described the Parisian crowds which played so prominent a role in the French revolution—*les sans-culottes, le peuple, la canaille, les bras-nus*—are all, for those who know the rules of the game, manifestos of a political affiliation and of a particular interpretation. Yet the historian is obliged to choose: the use of language forbids him to be neutral. Nor is it a matter of words alone. Over the past hundred years the changed balance of power in Europe has reversed the attitude of British historians to Frederick the Great. The changed balance of power within the Christian churches between Catholicism and Protestantism has profoundly altered their attitude to such figures as Loyola, Luther, and Cromwell. It requires only a superficial knowledge of the

work of French historians of the last forty years on the French revolution to recognize how deeply it has been affected by the Russian revolution of 1917. The historian belongs not to the past but to the present. Professor Trevor-Roper tells us that the historian "ought to love the past." [4] This is a dubious injunction. To love the past may easily be an expression of the nostalgic romanticism of old men and old societies, a symptom of loss of faith and interest in the present or future.[5] *Cliché* for *cliché*, I should prefer the one about freeing oneself from "the dead hand of the past." The function of the historian is neither to love the past nor to emancipate himself from the past, but to master and understand it as the key to the understanding of the present.

If, however, these are some of the insights of what I may call the Collingwood view of history, it is time to consider some of the dangers. The emphasis on the role of the historian in the making of history tends, if pressed to its logical conclusion, to rule out any objective history at all: history is what the historian makes. Collingwood seems indeed, at one moment, in

---

[4] Introduction to Burckhardt: *Judgments on History and Historians*, p. 17.

[5] Compare Nietzsche's view of history: "To old age belongs the old man's business of looking back and casting up his accounts, of seeking consolation in the memories of the past, in historical culture" (*Thoughts Out of Season* [London: Macmillan & Co.; 1909], II, pp. 65–6).

an unpublished note quoted by his editor, to have
reached this conclusion:

> St. Augustine looked at history from the point of
> view of the early Christian; Tillemont, from that of a
> seventeenth-century Frenchman; Gibbon, from that of an
> eighteenth-century Englishman; Mommsen, from that of
> a nineteenth-century German. There is no point in asking
> which was the right point of view. Each was the only one
> possible for the man who adopted it.[6]

This amounts to total scepticism, like Froude's remark
that history is "a child's box of letters with which we
can spell any word we please." [7] Collingwood, in his
reaction against "scissors-and-paste history," against
the view of history as a mere compilation of facts,
comes perilously near to treating history as something
spun out of the human brain, and leads back to the
conclusion referred to by Sir George Clark in the passage which I quoted earlier, that "there is no 'objective'
historical truth." In place of the theory that history
has no meaning, we are offered here the theory of an
infinity of meanings, none any more right than any
other—which comes to much the same thing. The
second theory is surely as untenable as the first. It does
not follow that, because a mountain appears to take on
different shapes from different angles of vision, it has
objectively either no shape at all or an infinity of

---

[6] Robin G. Collingwood: *The Idea of History* (London: Oxford
University Press; 1946), p. xii.

[7] James Anthony Froude: *Short Studies on Great Subjects*
(1894), I, p. 21.

shapes. It does not follow that, because interpretation plays a necessary part in establishing the facts of history, and because no existing interpretation is wholly objective, one interpretation is as good as another, and the facts of history are in principle not amenable to objective interpretation. I shall have to consider at a later stage what exactly is meant by objectivity in history.

But a still greater danger lurks in the Collingwood hypothesis. If the historian necessarily looks at his period of history through the eyes of his own time, and studies the problems of the past as a key to those of the present, will he not fall into a purely pragmatic view of the facts, and maintain that the criterion of a right interpretation is its suitability to some present purpose? On this hypothesis, the facts of history are nothing, interpretation is everything. Nietzsche had already enunciated the principle: "The falseness of an opinion is not for us any objection to it. . . . The question is how far it is life-furthering, life-preserving, species-preserving, perhaps species-creating." [8] The American pragmatists, moved, less explicitly and less wholeheartedly, along the same line. Knowledge is knowledge for some purpose. The validity of the knowledge depends on the validity of the purpose. But, even where no such theory has been professed, the practice has often been no less disquieting. In my own field of study I have seen too many examples of

---

[8] Froude: *Beyond Good and Evil*, Ch. i.

extravagant interpretation riding roughshod over facts, not to be impressed with the reality of this danger. It is not surprising that perusal of some of the more extreme products of Soviet and anti-Soviet schools of historiography should sometimes breed a certain nostalgia for that illusory nineteenth-century haven of purely factual history.

How then, in the middle of the twentieth century, are we to define the obligation of the historian to his facts? I trust that I have spent a sufficient number of hours in recent years chasing and perusing documents, and stuffing my historical narrative with properly footnoted facts, to escape the imputation of treating facts and documents too cavalierly. The duty of the historian to respect his facts is not exhausted by the obligation to see that his facts are accurate. He must seek to bring into the picture all known or knowable facts relevant, in one sense or another, to the theme on which he is engaged and to the interpretation proposed. If he seeks to depict the Victorian Englishman as a moral and rational being, he must not forget what happened at Stalybridge Wakes in 1850. But this, in turn, does not mean that he can eliminate interpretation, which is the life-blood of history. Laymen—that is to say, non-academic friends or friends from other academic disciplines—sometimes ask me how the historian goes to work when he writes history. The commonest assumption appears to be that the historian divides his work into two sharply distinguishable phases or periods. First, he spends a long preliminary period reading his sources and filling his notebooks with facts: then, when this is over, he puts away his sources, takes out his notebooks, and writes his book from beginning to end. This is to me an unconvincing and unplausible picture. For myself, as soon as I have got going on a few of what I take to be the capital sources, the itch becomes too strong and I begin to write—not necessarily at the beginning, but somewhere, anywhere. Thereafter, reading and writing go on simultaneously. The writing is added to, subtracted from, re-shaped, cancelled, as I go on reading. The reading is guided and directed and made fruitful by the writing: the more I write, the more I know what I am looking for, the better I understand the significance and relevance of what I find. Some historians probably do all this preliminary writing in their head without using pen, paper, or typewriter, just as some people play chess in their heads without recourse to board and chess-men: this is a talent which I envy, but cannot emulate. But I am convinced that, for any historian worth the name, the two processes of what economists call "input" and "output" go on simultaneously and are, in practice, parts of a single process. If you try to separate them, or to give one priority over the other, you fall into one of two heresies. Either you write scissors-and-paste history without meaning or significance; or you write propaganda or historical fiction, and merely use facts of the past to embroider a kind of writing which has nothing to do with history.

Our examination of the relation of the historian to

the facts of history finds us, therefore, in an apparently precarious situation, navigating delicately between the Scylla of an untenable theory of history as an objective compilation of facts, of the unqualified primacy of fact over interpretation, and the Charybdis of an equally untenable theory of history as the subjective product of the mind of the historian who establishes the facts of history and masters them through the process of interpretation, between a view of history having the centre of gravity in the past and the view having the centre of gravity in the present. But our situation is less precarious than it seems. We shall encounter the same dichotomy of fact and interpretation again in these lectures in other guises—the particular and the general, the empirical and the theoretical, the ob- jective and the subjective. The predicament of the historian is a reflexion of the nature of man. Man, except perhaps in earliest infancy and in extreme old age, is not totally involved in his environment and un- conditionally subject to it. On the other hand, he is never totally independent of it and its unconditional master. The relation of man to his environment is the relation of the historian to his theme. The historian is neither the humble slave, nor the tyrannical master, of his facts. The relation between the historian and his facts is one of equality, of give-and-take. As any work- ing historian knows, if he stops to reflect what he is doing as he thinks and writes, the historian is engaged on a continuous process of moulding his facts to his interpretation and his interpretation to his facts. It is impossible to assign primacy to one over the other.

The historian starts with a provisional selection of facts and a provisional interpretation in the light of which that selection has been made—by others as well as by himself. As he works, both the interpretation and the selection and ordering of facts undergo subtle and perhaps partly unconscious changes through the recip- rocal action of one or the other. And this reciprocal action also involves reciprocity between present and past, since the historian is part of the present and the facts belong to the past. The historian and the facts of history are necessary to one another. The historian without his facts is rootless and futile; the facts with- out their historian are dead and meaningless. My first answer therefore to the queston, What is history?, is that it is a continuous process of interaction between the historian and his facts, an unending dialogue be- tween the present and the past.

CHAPTER II

SOCIETY AND THE INDIVIDUAL

The question, which comes first—society or the individual—is like the question about the hen and the egg. Whether you treat it as a logical or as a historical question, you can make no statement about it, one way or the other, which does not have to be corrected by an opposite, and equally one-sided, statement. Society and the individual are inseparable; they are necessary and complementary to each other, not opposites. "No man is an island, entire of itself," in Donne's famous words; "every man is a piece of the continent, a part of the main." [1] That is an aspect of the truth. On the other hand, take the dictum of J. S. Mill, the classical individualist: "Men are not, when brought together, converted into another kind of substance." [2] Of course not. But the fallacy is to suppose that they existed, or had any kind of substance, before being "brought together." As soon as we are born, the world gets to work on us and transforms us from merely biological into social units. Every human being at every stage of history or pre-history is born into a society and from his earliest years is moulded by that society. The language which he speaks is not an individual inheritance, but

---

[1] *Devotions upon Emergent Occasions*, No. xvii.

[2] John Stuart Mill: *A System of Logic*, vii, 1.

a socal acquisition from the group in which he grows
up. Both language and environment help to determine
the character of his thought; his earliest ideas come to
him from others. As has been well said, the individual
apart from society would be both speechless and mind-
less. The lasting fascination of the Robinson Crusoe
myth is due to its attempt to imagine an individual
independent of society. The attempt breaks down.
Robinson is not an abstract individual, but an Englishman from New York; he carries his Bible with him
and prays to his tribal God. The myth quickly bestows
on him his Man Friday; and the building of a new society begins. The other relevant myth is that of
Kirillov in Dostoevsky's *Devils*, who kills himself in
order to demonstrate his perfect freedom. Suicide is
the only perfectly free act open to individual man;
every other act involves in one way or another his
membership in society.[3]

It is commonly said by anthropologists that primitive man is less individual and more completely
moulded by his society than civilized man. This contains an element of truth. Simpler societies are more
uniform in the sense that they call for, and provide
opportunities for, a far smaller diversity of individual
skills and occupations than the more complex and advanced societies. Increasing individualization in this

---

[3] Durkheim, in his well-known study of suicide, coined the word
anomie to denote the condition of the individual isolated from his
society—a state especially conducive to emotional disturbance and
suicide; but he also showed that suicide is by no means independent
of social conditions.

sense is a necessary product of modern advanced society, and runs through all its activities from top to
bottom. But it would be a serious error to set up an
antithesis between this process of individualization
and the growing strength and cohesion of society.
The development of society and the development
of the individual go hand in hand, and condition
each other. Indeed what we mean by a complex or
advanced society is a society in which the interdependence of individuals on one another has assumed advanced and complex forms. It would be
dangerous to assume that the power of a modern
national community to mould the character and
thought of its individual members, and to produce a
certain degree of conformity and uniformity among
them, is any less than that of a primitive tribal community. The old conception of national character
based on biological differences has long been exploded;
but differences of national character arising out of different national backgrounds of society and education
are difficult to deny. That elusive entity "human nature" has varied so much from country to country and
from century to century that it is difficult not to regard
it as a historical phenomenon shaped by prevailing social conditions and conventions. There are many differences between, say, Americans, Russians, and Indians. But some, and perhaps the most important, of
these differences take the form of different attitudes to
social relations between individuals, or, in other words,
to the way in which society should be constituted, so

that the study of differences between individual American, Russian, and Indian society as a whole may well turn out to be the best way of studying differences between individual Americans, Russians, and Indians. Civilized man, like primitive man, is moulded by society just as effectively as society is moulded by him. You can no more have the egg without the hen than you can have the hen without the egg.

It would have been unnecessary to dwell on these very obvious truths but for the fact that they have been obscured for us by the remarkable and exceptional period of history from which the Western world is only just emerging. The cult of individualism is one of the most pervasive of modern historical myths. According to the familiar account in Burckhardt's *Civilization of the Renaissance in Italy,* the second part of which is sub-titled "The Development of the Individual," the cult of the individual began with the Renaissance, when man, who had hitherto been "conscious of himself only as a member of a race, people, party, family, or corporation," at length "became a spiritual individual and recognized himself as such." Later the cult was connected with the rise of capitalism and of Protestantism, with the beginnings of the industrial revolution and with the doctrines of *laissez-faire.* The rights of man and the citizen proclaimed by the French revolution were the rights of the individual. Individualism was the basis of the great nineteenth-century philosophy of utilitarianism. Morley's essay "On Compromise," a characteristic document of Victorian liberalism, called individualism and utilitarianism "the religion of human happiness and well-being." "Rugged individualism" was the keynote of human progress. This may be a perfectly sound and valid analysis of the ideology of a particular historical epoch. But what I want to make clear is that the increased individualization which accompanied the rise of the modern world was a normal process of advancing civilization. A social revolution brought new social groups to positions of power. It operated as always through individuals and by offering fresh opportunities of individual development; and, since in the early stages of capitalism the units of production and distribution were largely in the hands of single individuals, the ideology of the new social order strongly emphasized the role of individual initiative in the social order. But the whole process was a social process representing a specific stage in historical development, and cannot be explained in terms of a revolt of individuals against society or of an emancipation of individuals from social restraints. Many signs suggest that even in the Western world, which was the focus of this development and of this ideology, this period of history has reached its end: I need not insist here on the rise of what is called mass democracy, or on the gradual replacement of predominantly individual by predominantly collective forms of economic production and organization. But the ideology generated by this long and fruitful period is still a dominant force in Western Europe and throughout the English-speaking countries. When we speak in abstract terms of the tension between liberty and equality, or between individual liberty and social justice, we are apt to forget that fights do not occur between abstract ideas. These are not struggles between individuals as such and society as such, but between groups of individuals in society, each group striving to promote social policies favourable to it and to frustrate social policies inimical to it. Individualism, in the sense no longer of a great social movement, but of false opposition between individual and society, has become today the slogan of an interested group and, because of its controversial character, a barrier to our understanding of what goes on in the world. I have nothing to say against the cult of the individual as a protest against the perversion which treats the individual as a means and society or the state as the end. But we shall arrive at no real understanding either of the past or of the present if we attempt to operate with the concept of an abstract individual standing outside society.

And this brings me at last to the point of my long digression. The common-sense view of history treats it as something written by individuals about individuals. This view was certainly taken and encouraged by nineteenth-century liberal historians, and is not in substance incorrect. But it now seems over-simplified and inadequate, and we need to probe deeper. The knowledge of the historian is not his exclusive individual possession: men, probably, of many generations and of many different countries have participated in accumulating it. The men whose actions the historian studies

were not isolated individuals acting in a vacuum: they
acted in the context, and under the impulse of a past
society. In my last lecture I described history as a process of interaction, a dialogue between the historian
in the present and the facts of the past. I now want to
enquire into the relative weight of the individual and
social elements on both sides of the equation. How far
are historians single individuals, and how far products
of their society and their period? How far are the facts
of history facts about single individuals and how far
social facts?

The historian, then, is an individual human being.
Like other individuals, he is also a social phenomenon,
both the product and the conscious or unconscious
spokesman of the society to which he belongs; it is
this capacity that he approaches the facts of the historical past. We sometimes speak of the course of
history as a "moving procession." The metaphor is fair
enough, provided it does not tempt the historian to
think of himself as an eagle surveying the scene from
a lonely crag or as a V.I.P. at the saluting base. Nothing of the kind! The historian is just another dim figure trudging along in another part of the procession.
And as the procession winds along, swerving now to
the right and now to the left, and sometimes doubling
back on itself, the relative positions of different parts
of the procession are constantly changing, so that it
may make perfectly good sense to say, for example,

that we are nearer today to the Middle Ages than were our great-grandfathers a century ago, or that the age of Caesar is nearer to us than the age of Dante. New vistas, new angles of vision, constantly appear as the procession—and the historian with it—moves along. The historian is part of history. The point in the procession at which he finds himself determines his angle of vision over the past.

This truism is no less true when the period treated by the historian is remote from his own time. When I studied ancient history, the classics on the subject were—and probably still are—Grote's *History of Greece* and Mommsen's *History of Rome*. Grote, an enlightened radical banker writing in the 1840's, embodied the aspirations of the rising and politically progressive British middle class in an idealized picture of Athenian democracy, in which Pericles figured as a Benthamite reformer, and Athens acquired an empire in a fit of absence of mind. It may not be fanciful to suggest that Grote's neglect of the problem of slavery in Athens reflected the failure of the group to which he belonged to face the problem of the new English factory working class. Mommsen was a German liberal, disillusioned by the muddles and humiliations of the German revolution of 1848–1849. Writing in the 1850's—the decade which saw the birth of the name and concept of *Realpolitik*—Mommsen was imbued with the sense of need for a strong man to clear up the mess left by the failure of the German people to realize its political aspirations; and we shall

never appreciate his history at its true value unless we
realize that his well-known idealization of Caesar is
the product of this yearning for the strong man to save
Germany from ruin, and that the lawyer-politician
Cicero, that ineffective chatterbox and slippery pro-
crastinator, has walked straight out of the debates of
the Paulikirche in Frankfurt in 1848. Indeed, I should
not think it an outrageous paradox if someone were to
say that Grote's *History of Greece* has quite as much
to tell us today about the thought of the English
philosophical radicals in the 1840's as about Athenian
democracy in the fifth century B.C., or that anyone
wishing to understand what 1848 did to the German
liberals should take Mommsen's *History of Rome* as
one of his text-books. Nor does this diminish their
stature as great historical works. I have no patience
with the fashion set by Bury in his inaugural lecture
of pretending that Mommsen's greatness rests not on
his *History of Rome,* but on his corpus of inscriptions
and his work on Roman constitutional law: this is to
reduce history to the level of compilation. Great history is written precisely when the historian's vision of
the past is illuminated by insights into the problems
of the present. Surprise has often been expressed that
Mommsen failed to continue his history beyond the
fall of the republic. He lacked neither time, nor opportunity nor knowledge. But, when Mommsen wrote
his history, the strong man had not yet arisen in Germany. During his active career, the problem of what
happened once the strong man had taken over was not

yet actual. Nothing inspired Mommsen to project this problem back on to the Roman scene; and the history of the empire remained unwritten.

It would be easy to multiply examples of this phenomenon among modern historians. In my last lecture I paid tribute to Dr. Trevelyan's *England under Queen Anne* as a monument to the Whig tradition in which he had been reared. Let us now consider the imposing and significant achievement of one whom most of us would regard as the greatest British historian to emerge on the academic scene since the First World War: Sir Lewis Namier. Namier was a true conservative—not a typical English conservative, who when scratched turns out to be 75 per cent liberal, but a conservative such as we have not seen among British historians for more than a hundred years. Between the middle of the last century and 1914 it was scarcely possible for a British historian to conceive of historical change except as change for the better. In the 1920's, we moved into a period in which change was beginning to be associated with fear for the future, and could be thought of as change for the worse—a period of the rebirth of conservative thinking. Like Acton's liberalism, Namier's conservatism derived both strength and profundity from being rooted in a continental background.[4] Unlike Fisher or Toynbee, Na-

---

[4] It is perhaps worth remarking that the only other considerable conservative British writer of the period between the wars, Mr. T. S. Eliot, also enjoyed the advantage of a non-British background; nobody brought up in Great Britain before 1914 could wholly escape the inhibiting influences of the liberal tradition.

mier had no roots in the nineteenth-century liberalism, and suffered from no nostalgic regrets for it. After the First World War and the abortive peace had revealed the bankruptcy of liberalism, the reaction would come only in one of two forms—socialism or conservatism. Namier appeared as the conservative historian. He worked in two chosen fields, and the choice of both was significant. In English history he went back to the last period in which the ruling class had been able to engage in the rational pursuit of position and power in an orderly and mainly static society. Somebody has accused Namier of taking mind out of history.[5] It is not perhaps a very fortunate phrase, but one can see the point which the critic was trying to make. Politics at the accession of George III were still immune from the fanaticism of ideas, and of that passionate belief in progress, which was to break on the world with the French revolution and usher in the century of triumphant liberalism. No ideas, no revolution, no liberalism: Namier chose to give us a brilliant portrait of an age still safe—though not to remain safe for long—from all these dangers.

But Namier's choice of a second subject was equally significant. Namier by-passed the great modern revolutions, English, French, and Russian—he wrote noth-

---

[5] The original criticism, in an anonymous article in *The Times Literary Supplement* of August 28, 1953, on "The Namier View of History" ran as follows: "Darwin was accused of taking mind out of the universe; and Sir Lewis has been the Darwin of political history—in more senses than one."

ing of substance on any of them—and elected to give
us a penetrating study of the European revolution of
1848—a revolution that failed, a set-back all over Europe for the rising hopes of liberalism, a demonstration
of the hollowness of ideas in face of armed force, of
democrats when confronted with soldiers. The intrusion of ideas into the serious business of politics is
futile and dangerous: Namier rubbed in the moral by
calling this humiliating failure "the revolution of the
intellectuals." Nor is our conclusion a matter of infer-
ence alone; for, though Namier wrote nothing systematic on the philosophy of history, he expressed himself,
with his usual clarity and incisiveness, in an essay published a few years ago. "The less, therefore," he
wrote, "man clogs the free play of his mind with political doctrine and dogma, the better for his thinking."
And, after mentioning, and not rejecting, the charge
that he had taken the mind out of history, he went on:

Some political philosophers complain of a "tired lull"
and the absence at present of argument on general politics
in this country; practical solutions are sought for concrete
problems, while programmes and ideals are forgotten by
both parties. But to me this attitude seems to betoken a
greater national maturity, and I can only wish that it may
long continue undisturbed by the workings of political
philosophy.[6]

I do not want at the moment to join issue with this
view: I will reserve that for a later lecture. My purpose

---

[6] Lewis Namier: *Personalities and Powers* (London: Hamish
Hamilton; 1955), pp. 5, 7.

here is merely to illustrate two important truths: first, that you cannot fully understand or appreciate the work of the historian unless you have first grasped the standpoint from which he himself approached it; second, that that standpoint is itself rooted in a social and historical background. Do not forget that, as Marx once said, the educator himself has to be educated; in modern jargon, the brain of the brain-washer has itself been washed. The historian, before he begins to write history, is the product of history.

The historians of whom I have just spoken—Grote and Mommsen, Trevelyan and Namier—were each of them cast, so to speak, in a single social and political mould; no marked change of outlook occurs between their earlier and later work. But some historians in periods of rapid change have reflected in their writings not one society and one social order, but a succession of different orders. The best example known to me of this is the great German historian Meinecke, whose span of life and work was unusually long, and covered with a series of revolutionary and catastrophic changes in the fortunes of his country. Here we have in effect three different Meineckes, each the spokesman of a different historical epoch, and each speaking through one of his three major works. The Meinecke of *Weltbürgerthum and Nationalstaat*, published in 1907, confidently sees the realization of German national ideals in the Bismarckian Reich and—like many nineteenth-century thinkers from Mazzini onwards—identifies nationalism with the highest form of universalism: this is the product of the baroque Wilhelmine sequel to the age of Bismarck. The Meinecke of *Die Idee der Staatsräson*, published in 1925, speaks with the divided and bewildered mind of the Weimar Republic: the world of politics has become an arena of unresolved conflict between *raison d'état* and morality which is external to politics, but which cannot in the last resort override the life and security of the state. Finally the Meinecke of *Die Entstehung des Historismus*, published in 1936, when he had been swept from his academic honours by the Nazi flood, utters a cry of despair, rejecting a historicism which appears to recognize that whatever is, is right, and tossing uneasily between the historical relative and a super-rational absolute. Last of all, when Meinecke in his old age had seen his country succumb to a military defeat more crushing than that of 1918, he relapsed helplessly in *Die Deutsche Katastrophe* of 1946 into the belief in a history at the mercy of blind, inexorable change.[7] The psychologist or the biographer would be interested here in Meinecke's development as an individual: what interests the historian is the way in which Meinecke reflects back three—or even four —successive, and sharply contrasted, periods of present time into the historical past.

Or let us take a distinguished example nearer home.

---

[7] I am indebted here to Dr. W. Stark's excellent analysis of Meinecke's development in his introduction to an English translation of *Die Idee der Staatsräson*, published under the title *Machiavellism* in 1957; Dr. Stark perhaps exaggerates the super-rational element in Meinecke's third period.

In the iconoclastic 1930's, when the Liberal Party had just been snuffed out as an effective force in British politics, Professor Butterfield wrote a book called *The Whig Interpretation of History*, which enjoyed a great and deserved success. It was a remarkable book in many ways—not least because, though it denounced the Whig interpretation over some 130 pages, it did not, so far as I can discover without the help of an index, name a single Whig except Fox, who was no historian, or a single historian save Acton, who was no Whig.[8] But anything that the book lacked in detail and precision it made up for in sparkling invective. The reader was left in no doubt that the Whig interpretation was a bad thing; and one of the charges brought against it was that it "studies the past with reference to the present." On this point Professor Butterfield was categorical and severe:

> The study of the past with one eye, so to speak, upon the present is the source of all sins and sophistries in history. . . . It is the essence of what we mean by the word "unhistorical."[9]

Twelve years elapsed. The fashion for iconoclasm went out. Professor Butterfield's country was engaged in war often said to be fought in defence of the constitutional liberties embodied in the Whig tradition, under a great leader who constantly invoked the past "with one eye,

---

[8] Butterfield: *The Whig Interpretation of History*. On p. 67 the author confesses to "a healthy sort of distrust" of "disembodied reasoning."

[9] Ibid., pp. 11, 31–2.

so to speak, upon the present." In a small book called *The Englishman and His History* published in 1944, Professor Butterfield not only decided that the Whig interpretation of history is the "English" interpretation, but spoke enthusiastically of "the Englishman's alliance with his history" and of the "marriage between the present and the past." [1] To draw attention to these reversals of outlook is not an unfriendly criticism. It is not my purpose to refute the proto-Butterfield with the deutero-Butterfield, or to confront Professor Butterfield drunk with Professor Butterfield sober. I am fully aware that, if anyone took the trouble to peruse some of the things I wrote before, during, and after the war, he would have no difficulty at all in convicting me of contradictions and inconsistencies at least as glaring as any I have detected in others. Indeed, I am not sure that I should envy any historian who could honestly claim to have lived through the earth-shaking events of the past fifty years without some radical modifications of his outlook. My purpose is merely to show how closely the work of the historian mirrors the society in which he works. It is not merely the events that are in flux. The historian himself is in flux. When you take up a historical work, it is not enough to look for the author's name in the title-page: look also for the date of publication or writing— it is sometimes even more revealing. If the philosopher is right in telling us that we cannot step into the same

---

[1] Butterfield: *The Englishman and His History* (Cambridge University Press; 1944), pp. 2, 4-5.

river twice, it is perhaps equally true, and for the same reason, that two books cannot be written by the same historian.

And if, moving for a moment from the individual historian to what may be called broad trends in historical writing, the extent to which the historian is the product of his society becomes all the more apparent. In the nineteenth century British historians with scarcely an exception regarded the course of history as a demonstration of the principle of progress: they expressed the ideology of a society in a condition of remarkably rapid progress. History was full of meaning for British historians, so long as it seemed to be going our way; now that it has taken a wrong turning, belief in the meaning of history has become a heresy. After the First World War, Toynbee made a desperate attempt to replace a linear view of history by a cyclical theory—the characteristic ideology of a society in decline.[2] Since Toynbee's failure, British historians have for the most part been content to throw in their hands and declare that there is no general pattern in history at all. A banal remark by Fisher to that effect[3] has achieved almost as wide a popularity as Ranke's aphorism in the last century. If anyone tells me that the British historians of the last thirty years experienced

---

[2] Marcus Aurelius in the twilight of the Roman Empire consoled himself by reflecting "how all things that are now happening have happened in the past, and will happen in the future" (*To Himself*, x, 27); as is well known, Toynbee took the idea from Spengler's *Decline of the West*.

[3] Preface, dated December 4, 1934, to *A History of Europe*.

this change of heart as the result of profound individual reflexion and of the burning of midnight oil in their separate garrets, I shall not think it necessary to contest the fact. But I shall continue to regard all this individual thinking and oil-burning as a social phenomenon, the product and expression of a fundamental change in the character and outlook of our society since 1914. There is no more significant pointer to the character of a society than the kind of history it writes or fails to write. Geyl, the Dutch historian, in his fascinating monograph translated into English under the title *Napoleon: For and Against,* shows how the successive judgments of French nineteenth-century historians on Napoleon reflected the changing and conflicting patterns of French political life and thought throughout the century. The thought of historians, as of other human beings, is moulded by the environment of the time and place. Acton, who fully recognized this truth, sought for an escape from it in history itself:

History must be our deliverer not only from the undue influence of other times, but from the undue influence of our own, from the tyranny of environment and the pressure of the air we breathe.[4]

This may sound too optimistic an assessment of the role of history. But I shall venture to believe that the historian who is most conscious of his own situation is also more capable of transcending it, and more ca-

---

[4] Acton: *Lectures on Modern History,* p. 33.

pable of appreciating the essential nature of the differences between his own society and outlook and those of other periods and other countries, than the historian who loudly protests that he is an individual and not a social phenomenon. Man's capacity to rise above his social and historical situation seems to be conditioned by the sensitivity with which he recognizes the extent of his involvement in it.

In my first lecture I said: Before you study the history, study the historian. Now I would add: Before you study the historian, study his historical and social environment. The historian, being an individual, is also a product of history and of society; and it is in this twofold light that the student of history must learn to regard him.

Let us now leave the historian and consider the other side of my equation—the facts of history—in the light of the same problem. Is the object of the historian's enquiry the behaviour of individuals or the action of social forces? Here I am moving on to well-trodden ground. When Sir Isaiah Berlin published a few years ago a sparkling and popular essay entitled *Historical Inevitability*—to the main thesis of which I shall return later in these lectures—he headed it with a motto culled from the works of Mr. T. S. Eliot "Vast impersonal forces"; and throughout the essay he pokes fun at people who believe in "vast impersonal forces" rather than individuals as the decisive factor in history. What I will call the Bad King John theory of history—the view that what matters in history is the character and behavior of individuals—has a long pedigree. The desire to postulate individual genius as the creative force in history is characteristic of the primitive stages of historical consciousness. The ancient Greeks liked to label the achievements of the past with the names of eponymous heroes supposedly responsible for them, to attribute their epics to a bard called Homer, and their laws and institutions to a Lycurgus or a Solon. The same inclination reappears at the Renaissance when Plutarch, the biographer-moralist, was much more popular and influential a figure in the classical revival than the historians of antiquity. In this country, in particular, we all learned this theory, so to speak, at our mother's knee; and today we should probably recognize that there is something childish, or at any rate childlike, about it. It had some plausibility in days when society was simpler, and public affairs appeared to be run by a handful of known individuals. It clearly does not fit the more complex society of our times; and the birth in the nineteenth century of the new science of sociology was a response to this growing complexity. Yet the old tradition dies hard. At the beginning of this century, "history is the biography of great men" was still a reputable dictum. Only ten years ago a distinguished American historian accused his colleagues, perhaps not too seriously, of the "mass murder of historical characters" by treating them as "puppets of social and economic forces." [5] Addicts of this theory tend nowadays to be shy about it; but, after some searching, I found an excellent contemporary statement of it in the introduction to one of Miss Wedgwood's books:

> The behaviour of men as individuals is more interesting to me than their behaviour as groups or classes. History can be written with this bias as well as another; it is neither more, nor less, misleading. . . . This book . . . is an attempt to understand how these men felt and why, in their own estimation, they acted as they did.[6]

This statement is precise; and, since Miss Wedgwood is a popular writer, many people, I am sure, think as she does. Dr. Rowse tells us, for instance, that the Elizabethan system broke down because James I was incapable of understanding it, and that the English revolution of the seventeenth century was an "accidental" event due to the stupidity of the two first Stuart kings.[7] Even Sir James Neale, a more austere historian than Dr. Rowse, sometimes seems more eager to express his admiration for Queen Elizabeth

---

[5] *American Historical Review*, Vol. LXI, No. 1 (January 1951), p. 270.

[6] Cicely Veronica Wedgwood: *The King's Peace* (London: William Collins Sons & Co.; 1955), p. 17.

[7] Alfred L. Rowse: *The England of Elizabeth* (London: Macmillan & Co.; 1950), pp. 261–2, 382. It is fair to point out that in an earlier essay Dr. Rowse condemned "historians who think that the Bourbons failed to re-establish the monarchy in France after 1870 just because of Henry V's attachment to a little white flag" (*The End of an Epoch*, p. 275); perhaps he reserves such personal explanations for English history.

than to explain what the Tudor monarchy stood for; and Sir Isaiah Berlin, in the essay which I have just quoted, is terribly worried by the prospect that historians may fail to denounce Genghis Khan and Hitler as bad men.[8] The Bad King John and Good Queen Bess theory is especially rife when we come to more recent times. It is easier to call Communism "the brain-child of Karl Marx" (I pluck this flower from a recent stockbrokers' circular) than to analyse its origin and character, to attribute the Bolshevik revolution to the stupidity of Nicholas II or to German gold than to study its profound social causes, and to see in the two world wars of this century the result of the individual wickedness of Wilheim II and Hitler rather than of some deep-seated breakdown in the system of international relations.

Miss Wedgwood's statement, then, combines two propositions. The first is that the behaviour of men as individuals is distinct from their behaviour as members of groups or classes, and that the historian may legitimately choose to dwell on the one rather than on the other. The second is that the study of the behaviour of men as individuals consists of the study of the conscious motives of their actions.

After what I have already said, I need not labour the first point. It is not that the view of man as an individual is more or less misleading than the view of him as a member of the group; it is the attempt to

---

[8] Isaiah Berlin: *Historical Inevitability* (London: Oxford University Press; 1954), p. 42.

draw a distinction between the two which is misleading. The individual is by definition a member of a
society, or probably of more than one society—call it
group, class, tribe, nation, or what you will. Early biologists were content to classify species of birds,
beasts, and fishes in cages, aquariums, and showcases,
and did not seek to study the living creature in relation to its environment. Perhaps the social sciences
today have not yet fully emerged from that primitive
stage. Some people distinguish between psychology as
the science of the individual and sociology as the science of society; and the name "psychologism has been
given to the view that all social problems are ultimately reducible to the analysis of individual human
behaviour. But the psychologist who failed to study
the social environment of the individual would not
get very far.[9] It is tempting to make a distinction between biography, which treats man as an individual,
and history, which treats man as part of a whole, and
to suggest that good biography makes bad history.
"Nothing causes more error and unfairness in man's
view of history," Acton once wrote, "than the interest

---

[9] Modern psychologists have none the less been convicted of this
error: "Psychologists as a group have not treated the individual as a
unit *in* a functioning social system, but rather as the concrete
human being who was then conceived as proceeding to form social
systems. They have thus not adequately taken account of the
peculiar sense in which their categories are abstract" (Professor
Talcott Parsons in the introduction to Max Weber: *The Theory of
Social and Economic Organization* [New York: Oxford University
Press; 1947], p. 27); see also the remarks on Freud, p. 184.

which is inspired by individual characters." [1] But this distinction, too, is unreal. Nor do I want to take shelter behind the Victorian proverb placed by G. M. Young on the title-page of his book *Victorian England*: "Servants talk about people, gentlefolk discuss things." [2] Some biographies are contributions to history—in my own field, Isaac Deutscher's biographies of Stalin and Trotsky are outstanding examples. Others belong to literature, like the historical novel. "To Lytton Strachey," writes Professor Trevor-Roper, "historical problems were always, and only, problems of individual behavior and individual eccentricity. . . . Historical problems, the problems of politics and society, he never sought to answer, or even to ask." [3] Nobody is obliged to write or read history; and excellent books can be written about the past which are not history. But I think we are entitled by convention—as I propose to do in these lectures—to reserve the word "history" for the serious process of enquiry into the past of man in society.

---

[1] *Home and Foreign Review* (January 1863), p. 219.

[2] This idea was elaborated by Herbert Spencer in his most solemn style in *The Study of Sociology*, Ch. 2: "If you want roughly to estimate anyone's mental calibre, you cannot do it better than by observing the ratio of generalities to personalities in his talk—how far simple truths about individuals are replaced by truths abstracted from numerous experiences of men and things. And when you have thus measured many, you find but a scattered few likely to take anything more than a biographical view of human affairs."

[3] Hugh Redwald Trevor-Roper: *Historical Essays* (London: Macmillan & Co.; 1957), p. 281.

The second point, *i.e.* that history is concerned to enquire why individuals, "in their own estimation, acted as they did," seems at first sight extremely odd; and I suspect that Miss Wedgwood, like other sensible people, does not practise what she preaches. If she does, she must write some very queer history. Everyone knows today that human beings do not always, or perhaps even habitually, act from motives of which they are fully conscious or which they are willing to avow; and to exclude insight into unconscious or unavowed motives is surely a way of going about one's work with one eye wilfully shut. This is, however, what, according to some people, historians ought to do. The point is this. So long as you are content to say that the badness of King John consisted in his greed or stupidity or ambition to play the tyrant, you are speaking in terms of individual qualities which are comprehensible even at the level of nursery history. But, once you begin to say that King John was the unconscious tool of vested interests opposed to the rise to power of the feudal barons, you not only introduce a more complicated and sophisticated view of King John's badness, but you appear to suggest that historical events are determined not by the conscious actions of individuals, but by some extraneous and all-powerful forces guiding their unconscious will. This is, of course, nonsense. So far as I am concerned, I have no belief in divine providence, world spirit, manifest destiny, history with a capital H, or any other of the abstractions which have sometimes been sup-

posed to guide the course of events; and I should en-
dorse without qualification the comment of Marx:

> *History* does nothing, it possesses no immense wealth,
> fights no battles. It is rather *man*, real living *man* who
> does everything, who possesses and fights.[4]

The two remarks which I have to make on this question have nothing to do with any abstract view of history, and are based on purely empirical observation.

The first is that history is to a considerable extent
a matter of numbers. Carlyle was responsible for the
unfortunate assertion that "history is the biography
of great men." But listen to him at his most eloquent
and in his greatest historical work:

> Hunger and nakedness and righteous oppression lying
> heavy on 25 million hearts: this, not the wounded vanities
> or contradicted philosophies of philosophical advocates,
> rich shopkeepers, rural noblesse, was the prime mover in
> the French revolution; as the like will be in all such revo-
> lutions, in all countries.[5]

Or, as Lenin said, "politics begin where the masses
are, not where there are thousands, but where there
are millions, that is where serious politics begin." [6]
Carlyle's and Lenin's millions were millions of individuals: there was nothing impersonal about them.
Discussions of this question sometimes confuse ano-
nymity with impersonality. People do not cease to be
people, or individuals individuals, because we do not

---

[4] *Marx-Engels: Gesamtausgabe*, I, iii, 625.
[5] *History of the French Revolution*, III, iii, Ch. 1.
[6] Lenin: *Selected Works*, vii, 295.

know their names. Mr. Eliot's "vast, impersonal forces" were the individuals whom Clarendon, a bolder and franker conservative, calls "dirty people of no name." [7] These nameless millions were individuals acting, more or less unconsciously, together and constituting a social force. The historian will not in ordinary circumstances need to take cognizance of a single discontented peasant or discontented village. But millions of discontented peasants in thousands of villages are a factor which no historian will ignore. The reasons which deter Jones from getting married do not interest the historian unless the same reasons also deter thousands of other individuals of Jones's generation, and bring about a substantial fall in a marriage-rate: in that event, they may well be historically significant. Nor need we be perturbed by the platitude that movements are started by minorities. All effective movements have few leaders and a multitude of followers; but this does not mean that the multitude is not essential to their success. Numbers count in history.

My second observation is even better attested. Writers of many different schools of thought have concurred in remarking that the actions of individual human beings often have results which were not intended or desired by the actors or indeed by any other individual. The Christian believes that the individual,

---

[7] Clarendon: *A Brief View & Survey of the Dangerous & Pernicious Errors to Church & State in Mr. Hobbe's Book entitled Leviathan* (1676), p. 320.

acting consciously for his own often selfish ends, is the unconscious agent of God's purpose. Mandeville's "private vices—public benefits" was an early and deliberately paradoxical expression of this discovery. Adam Smith's hidden hand and Hegel's "cunning of reason," which sets individuals to work for it and to serve its purposes, though the individuals believe themselves to be fulfilling their own personal desires, are too familiar to require quotation. "In the social production of their means of production," wrote Marx in the preface to his *Critique of Political Economy*, "human beings enter into definite and necessary relations which are independent of their will." "Man lives consciously for himself," wrote Tolstoy in *War and Peace*, echoing Adam Smith, "but is an unconscious instrument in the attainment of the historic, universal aims of humanity." [8] And here, to round off this anthology, which is already long enough, is Professor Butterfield: "There is something in the nature of historical events which twists the course of history in a direction that no man ever intended." [9] Since 1914, after a hundred years of only minor local wars, we have had two major world wars. It would not be a plausible explanation of this phenomenon to maintain that more individuals wanted war, or fewer wanted peace, in the first half of the twentieth century than in the last three quarters of the nineteenth. It is difficult to believe that any individual willed or

---

[8] Leo Tolstoy: *War and Peace*, ix, Ch. 1.

[9] Butterfield: *The Englishman and His History*, p. 103.

desired the great economic depression of the 1930's. Yet it was indubitably brought about by the actions of individuals, each consciously pursuing some totally different aim. Nor does the diagnosis of a discrepancy between the intentions of the individual and the results of his action always have to wait for the retrospective historian. "He does not mean to go to war," wrote Lodge of Woodrow Wilson in March 1917, "but I think he will be carried away by events." [1] It defies all the evidence to suggest that history can be written on the basis of "explanations in terms of human intentions" [2] or of accounts of their motives given by the actors themselves, of why, "in their own estimation, they acted as they did." The facts of history are indeed facts about individuals, but not about actions of individuals performed in isolation, and not about the motives, real or imaginary, from which individuals suppose themselves to have acted. They are facts about the relations of individuals to one another in society and about the social forces which produce from the actions of individuals results often at variance with, and sometimes opposite to, the results which they themselves intended.

One of the serious errors of Collingwood's view of history which I discussed in my last lecture was to assume that the thought behind the act, which the his-

---

[1] Quoted in Barbara Wertheim Tuchman: *The Zimmermann Telegram* (New York: Viking Press; 1958), p. 180.

[2] The phrase is quoted from Berlin: *Historical Inevitability*, p. 7, where the writing of history in these terms appears to be commended.

torian was called on to investigate, was the thought
of the individual actor. This is a false assumption.
What the historian is called on to investigate is what
lies behind the act; and to this the conscious thought
or motive of the individual actor may be quite irrelevant.

Here I should say something about the role of the
rebel or dissident in history. To set up the popular
picture of the individual in revolt against society is to
re-introduce the false antithesis between society and
the individual. No society is fully homogeneous. Every society is an arena of social conflicts, and those
individuals who range themselves against existing authority are no less products and reflexions of the society than those who uphold it. Richard II and Catherine the Great represented powerful social forces in
the England of the fourteenth century and in the Russia of the eighteenth century: but so also did Wat
Tyler and Pugachev, the leaders of the great serf re-
bellions. Monarchs and rebels alike were the product
of the specific conditions of their age and country.
To describe Wat Tyler and Pugachev as individuals
in revolt against society is a misleading simplification.
If they had been merely that, the historian would
never have heard of them. They owe their role in history to the mass of their followers, and are significant
as social phenomena, or not at all. Or let us take an
outstanding rebel and individualist at a more sophisticated level. Few people have reacted more violently
and more radically against the society of their day and

country than Nietzsche. Yet Nietzsche was a direct product of European, and more specifically of German, society—a phenomenon which could not have occurred in China or Peru. A generation after Nietzsche's death it became clearer than it had been to his contemporaries how strong were the European, and specifically German, social forces of which this individual had been the expression; and Nietzsche became a more significant figure for posterity than for his own generation.

The role of the rebel in history has some analogies with that of the great man. The great man theory of history—a particular example of the Good Queen Bess school—has gone out of fashion in recent years, though it still occasionally rears its ungainly head. The editor of a series of popular history text-books started after the Second World War invited his authors "to open up a significant historical theme by way of a biography of a great man"; and Mr. A. J. P. Taylor told us in one of his minor essays that "the history of modern Europe can be written in terms of three titans: Napoleon, Bismarck, and Lenin," [3] though in his more serious writings he has undertaken no such rash project. What is the role of the great man in history? The great man is an individual and, being an outstanding individual, is also a social phenomenon of outstanding importance. "It is an obvious truth," observed Gibbon, "that the times must be suited to extraordinary

[3] A. J. P. Taylor: *From Napoleon to Stalin* (London: Hamish Hamilton; 1950), p. 74.

characters, and that the genius of Cromwell or Retz might now expire in obscurity." [4] Marx in *The Eighteenth Brumaire of Louis Bonaparte* diagnosed the converse phenomenon: "The class war in France created circumstances and relations which enabled a gross mediocrity to strut about in a hero's garb." Had Bismarck been born in the eighteenth century—an absurd hypothesis, since he would not then have been Bismarck—he would not have united Germany, and might not have been a great man at all. But one need not, I think, as Tolstoy does, decry great men as no more than "labels giving names to events." Sometimes of course the cult of the great man may have sinister implications. Nietzsche's superman is a repellant figure. It is not necessary for me to recall the case of Hitler, or the grim consequences of the "cult of personality" in the Soviet Union. But it is not my purpose to deflate the greatness of great men: nor do I want to subscribe to the thesis that "great men are almost always bad men." The view which I would hope to discourage is the view which places great men outside history and sees them as imposing themselves on history in virtue of their greatness, "as jack-in-the-boxes who emerge miraculously from the unknown to interrupt the real continuity of history." [5] Even today I do not know that we can better Hegel's classic description:

---

[4] Gibbon: *The Decline and Fall of the Roman Empire*, Ch. lxx.
[5] V. Gordon Childe: *History* (London: Cobbett Press; 1947), p. 43.

The great man of the age is the one who can put into words the will of his age, tell his age what its will is, and accomplish it. What he does is the heart and essence of his age; he actualizes his age.[6]

Dr. Leavis means something like this when he says that great writers are "significant in terms of the human awareness they promote."[7] The great man is always representative either of existing forces or of forces which he helps to create by way of challenge to existing authority. But the higher degree of creativity may perhaps be assigned to those great men who, like Cromwell or Lenin, helped to mould the forces which carried them to greatness, rather than to those who, like Napoleon or Bismarck, rode to greatness on the back of already existing forces. Nor should we forget those great men who stood so far in advance of their own time that their greatness was recognized only by succeeding generations. What seems to me essential is to recognize in the great man an outstanding individual who is at once a product and an agent of the historical process, at once the representative and the creator of social forces which change the shape of the world and the thoughts of men.

History, then, in both senses of the word—meaning both the enquiry conducted by the historian and the facts of the past into which he enquires—is a social

---

[6] *Philosophy of Right* (London: Oxford University Press; 1942), p. 295.

[7] Frank R. Leavis: *The Great Tradition* (London: Chatto & Windus; 1948), p. 2.

process, in which individuals are engaged as social beings; and the imaginary antithesis between society and the individual is no more than a red herring drawn across our path to confuse our thinking. The reciprocal process of interaction between the historian and his facts, what I have called the dialogue between present and past, is a dialogue not between abstract and isolated individuals, but between the society of today and the society of yesterday. History, in Burckhardt's words, is "the record of what one age finds worthy of note in another." [8] The past is intelligible to us only in the light of the present; and we can fully understand the present only in the light of the past. To enable man to understand the society of the past and to increase his mastery over the society of the present is the dual function of history.

---

[8] Burckhardt: *Judgments on History and Historians*, p. 158.

CHAPTER III

HISTORY, SCIENCE, AND MORALITY

WHEN I was very young, I was suitably impressed to learn that, appearances notwithstanding, the whale is not a fish. Nowadays these questions of classification move me less; and it does not worry me unduly when I am assured that history is not a science. This terminological question is an eccentricity of the English language. In every other European language, the equivalent word to "science" includes history without hesitation. But in the English-speaking world this question has a long past behind it, and the issues raised by it are a convenient introduction to the problems of method in history.

At the end of the eighteenth century, when science had contributed so triumphantly both to man's knowledge of the world and to man's knowledge of his own physical attributes, it began to be asked whether science could not also further man's knowledge of society. The conception of the social sciences, and of history among them, gradually developed throughout the nineteenth century; and the method by which science studied the world of nature was applied to the study of human affairs. In the first part of this period the Newtonian tradition prevailed. Society, like the world of nature, was thought of as a mechanism; the title of a work by Herbert Spencer, *Social Statics*, published in 1851, is still remembered. Bertrand Russell, reared in this tradition, later recalled the period when he hoped that in time there would be "a mathematics of human behaviour as precise as the mathematics of machines." [1] Then Darwin made another scientific revolution; and social scientists, taking their cue from biology, began to think of society as an organism. But the real importance of the Darwinian revolution was that Darwin, completing what Lyell had already begun in geology, brought history into science. Science was concerned no longer with something static and timeless,[2] but with a process of change and development. Evolution in science confirmed and complemented progress in history. Nothing, however, occurred to alter the inductive view of historical method which I described in my first lecture: first collect your facts, then interpret them. It was assumed without question that this was also the method of science. This was the view which Bury evidently had in mind when, in the closing words of his inaugural lecture of January 1903, he described history as "a science, no more and no less." The fifty years after Bury's inaugural witnessed a strong reaction against this view of history. Collingwood, when he wrote in the 1930's, was

---

[1] Bertrand Russell: *Portraits from Memory* (London: George Allen & Unwin; 1956, p. 20.

[2] As late as 1874, Bradley distinguished science from history as being concerned with the timeless and "abiding" (F. H. Bradley: *Collected Essays* [London: Oxford University Press; 1935], I, p. 36).

particularly anxious to draw a sharp line between the
world of nature, which was the object of scientific
enquiry, and the world of history; and during this
period Bury's dictum was rarely quoted except in
terms of derision. But what historians failed to notice
at the time was that science itself had undergone a
profound revolution, which makes it seem that Bury
may have been more nearly right than we had supposed, though for the wrong reason. What Lyell did
for geology and Darwin for biology has now been done
for astronomy, which has become a science of how
the universe came to be what it is; and modern physicists constantly tell us that what they investigate are
not facts, but events. The historian has some excuse
for feeling himself more at home in the world of science today than he could have done a hundred years
ago.

Let us look first at the concept of laws. Throughout
the eighteenth and nineteenth centuries, scientists assumed that laws of nature—Newton's laws of motion,
the law of gravitation, Boyle's law, the law of evolution, and so forth—had been discovered and definitely
established, and that the business of the scientist was
to discover and establish more such laws by process of
induction from observed facts. The word "law" came
down trailing clouds of glory from Galileo and Newton. Students of society, consciously or unconsciously
desiring to assert the scientific status of their studies,
adopted the same language and believed themselves to
be following the same procedure. The political econo-

mists seem to have been first in the field with Gresham's law, and Adam Smith's laws of the market. Burke appealed to "the laws of commerce, which are the laws of nature, and consequently the Laws of God." [3] Malthus propounded a law of population; Lassalle an iron law of wages; and Marx in the preface to *Capital* claimed to have discovered "the economic law of motion of modern society." Buckle in the concluding words of his *History of Civilization* expressed the conviction that the course of human affairs was "permeated by one glorious principle of universal and undeviating regularity." Today this terminology sounds as old-fashioned as it is presumptuous; but it sounds almost as old-fashioned to the physical scientist as it does to the social scientist. In the year before Bury delivered his inaugural lecture, the French mathematician Henri Poincaré published a small volume called *La Science et l'hypothèse* which started a revolution in scientific thinking. Poincaré's main thesis was that the general propositions enunciated by scientists, where they were not mere definitions or disguised conventions about the use of language, were hypotheses designed to crystallize and organize further thinking, and were subject to verification, modification, or refutation. All this has now become something of a com-

---

[3] *Thoughts and Details on Scarcity* (1795) in *The Works of Edmund Burke* (1846), iv, p. 270. Burke deduced that it was not "within the competence of the government, taken as government, or even of the rich, as rich, to supply to the poor those necessaries which it has pleased the Divine Providence for awhile to withhold from them."

monplace. Newton's boast "Hypotheses non fingo"
rings hollow today; and though scientists, and even
social scientists, still sometimes refer to laws, so to
speak, for old time's sake, they no longer believe in
their existence in the sense in which scientists of the
eighteenth and nineteenth century universally believed
in them. It is recognized that scientists make discoveries and acquire fresh knowledge, not by establishing
precise and comprehensive laws, but by enunciating
hypotheses which open the way to fresh enquiry. A
standard text-book on scientific method by two American philosophers describes the method of science as
"essentially circular":

> We obtain evidence for principles by appealing to em-
> pirical material, to what is alleged to be "fact"; and we
> select, analyse, and interpret empirical material on the
> basis of principles.[4]

The word "reciprocal" would perhaps have been preferable to "circular"; for the result is not to return to
the same place, but to move forward to fresh discoveries through this process of interaction between principles and facts, between theory and practice. All
thinking requires acceptance of certain presuppositions based on observation which make scientific
thinking possible but are subject to revision in the
light of that thinking. These hypotheses may well be
valid in some contexts for some purposes, though they

---

[4] Morris Raphael Cohen and Ernest Nagel: *Introduction to Logic
and Scientific Method* (New York: Harcourt Brace & Company;
1934), p. 596.

turn out to be invalid in others. The test in all cases is the empirical one whether they are in fact effective in promoting fresh insights and adding to our knowledge. The methods of Rutherford were recently described by one of his most distinguished pupils and fellow-workers:

> He had a driving urge to know how nuclear phenomena worked in the sense in which one could speak of knowing what went on in the kitchen. I do not believe that he searched for an explanation in the classical manner of a theory using certain basic laws; as long as he knew what was happening he was content.[5]

This description equally fits the historian, who has abandoned the search for basic laws and is content to enquire how things work.

The status of the hypotheses used by the historian in the process of his enquiry seems remarkably similar to that of the hypotheses used by the scientist. Take, for example, Max Weber's famous diagnosis of a relation between Protestantism and capitalism. Nobody today would call this a law, though it might have been hailed as such in an earlier period. It is a hypothesis which, though modified to some extent in the course of the enquiries which it inspired, has beyond doubt enlarged our understanding of both these movements. Or take a statement like that of Marx: "The hand-mill gives us a society with a feudal lord; the steam-mill

---

[5] Sir Charles Ellis in *Trinity Review* (Cambridge, Lent Term, 1960), p. 14.

gives us a society with an industrial capitalist." [6] This
is not in modern terminology a law, though Marx
would probably have claimed it as such, but a fruitful
hypothesis pointing the way to further enquiry and
fresh understanding. Such hypotheses are indispensable tools of thought. The well-known German
economist of the early 1900's, Werner Sombart, con-
fessed to a "troubled feeling" which overtook those
who had abandoned Marxism:

> When we lose the comfortable formulas that have
> hitherto been our guides amid the complexities of exist-
> ence . . . we feel like drowning in the ocean of facts un-
> til we find a new foothold or learn to swim. [7]

The controversy about periodization in history falls
into the category. The division of history into periods
is not a fact, but a necessary hypothesis or tool of
thought, valid in so far as it is illuminating, and dependent for its validity on interpretation. Historians
who differ on the question of when the Middle Ages
ended differ in their interpretation of certain events.
The question is not a question of fact; but it is also
not meaningless. The division of history into geographical sectors is equally not a fact, but a hypothesis: to speak of European history may be a valid and
fruitful hypothesis in some contexts, misleading and

---

[6] Marx and Engels: Gesamtausgabe I, vi, 179.

[7] W. Sombart: The Quintessence of Capitalism (London: George
Allen & Unwin; 1915), p. 354.

mischievous in others. Most historians assume that Russia is part of Europe; some passionately deny it. The bias of the historian can be judged by the hypothesis which he adopts. I must quote one general pronouncement on the methods of social science, since it comes from a great social scientist who was trained as a physical scientist. Georges Sorel, who practised as an engineer before he began in his forties to write about the problems of society, emphasized the need to isolate particular elements in a situation even at the risk of over-simplifying:

> One should proceed by feeling one's way; one should try out probable and partial hypotheses, and be satisfied with provisional approximations so as always to leave the door open to progressive correction.[8]

This is a far cry from the nineteenth century, when scientists, and historians like Acton, looked forward to one day establishing, through the accumulation of well-attested facts, a comprehensive body of knowledge which would settle all disputed issues once for all. Nowadays both scientists and historians entertain the more modest hope of advancing progressively from one fragmentary hypothesis to another, isolating their facts through the medium of their interpretations, and testing their interpretations by the facts; and the ways in which they go about it do not seem to me essen-

---

[8] G. Sorel: *Matériaux d'une théorie du prolétariat* (1919), p. 7.

tially different. In my first lecture I quoted a remark of Professor Barraclough that history was "not factual at all, but a series of accepted judgments." While I was preparing these lectures, a physicist from this university, in a B.B.C. broadcast, defined a scientific truth as "a statement which has been publicly accepted by the experts." [9] Neither of these formulas is entirely satisfactory—for reasons which will appear when I come to discuss the question of objectivity. But it was striking to find a historian and a physicist independently formulating the same problem in almost exactly the same words.

Analogies are, however, a notorious trap for the unwary: and I want to consider repectfully the arguments for believing that, great as are the differences between the mathematical and the natural sciences, or between different sciences within these categories, a fundamental distinction can be drawn between these sciences and history, and that this distinction makes it misleading to call history—and perhaps also the other so-called social sciences—by the name of science. These objections—some of them more convincing than others—are in brief: (1) that history deals exclusively with the unique, science with the general; (2) that history teaches no lessons; (3) that history is unable to predict; (4) that history is necessarily subjective, since man is observing himself; and (5) that history, unlike science, involves issues of religion and

---

[9] J. Ziman in *The Listener* (August 18, 1960).

morality. I will try to examine each of these points in turn.

First, it is alleged that history deals with the unique and particular, and science with the general and universal. This view may be said to start with Aristotle, who declared that poetry was "more philosophical" and "more serious" than history, since poetry was concerned with general truth and history with particular.[1] A host of later writers, down to Collingwood [2] inclusive, made a similar distinction between science and history. This seems to rest on a misunderstanding. Hobbes' famous dictum still stands: "Nothing in the world is universal but names, for the things named are every one of them individual and singular." [3] This is certainly true of the physical sciences: no two geological formations, no two animals of the same species, and no two atoms, are identical. Similarly, no two historical events are identical. But insistence on the uniqueness of historical events has the same paralysing effect as the platitude taken over by Moore from Bishop Butler and at one time especially beloved by linguistic philosophers: "Everything is what it is and not another thing." Embarked on this course, you soon attain a sort of philosophical *nirvana*, in which nothing that matters can be said about anything.

---

[1] *Poetics*, Ch. ix.
[2] Collingwood: *Historical Imagination* (London: Oxford University Press; 1935), p. 5.
[3] *Leviathan*, I, iv.

The very use of language commits the historian, like the scientist, to generalization. The Peloponnesian War and the Second World War were very different, and both were unique. But the historian calls them both wars, and only the pedant will protest. When Gibbon wrote of both the establishment of Christianity by Constantine and the rise of Islam as revolutions,[4] he was generalizing two unique events. Modern historians do the same when they write of the English, French, Russian, and Chinese revolutions. The historian is not really interested in the unique, but in what is general in the unique. In the 1920's discussions by historians of the causes of the war of 1914 usually proceeded on the assumption that it was due either to the mismanagement of diplomats, working in secret and uncontrolled by public opinion, or to the unfortunate division of the world into territorial sovereign states. In the 1930's discussions proceeded on the assumption that it was due to rivalries between the imperialist powers driven by the stresses of capitalism in decline to partition the world between them. These discussions all involved generalizations about the causes of war, or at any rate of war in twentieth-century conditions. The historian constantly uses generalization to test his evidence. If the evidence is not clear whether Richard murdered the princes in the Tower, the historian will ask himself—perhaps unconsciously rather than con-

---

[4] *Decline and Fall of the Roman Empire*, Ch. xx, 1.

sciously—whether it was a habit of rulers of the period to liquidate potential rivals to their throne; and his judgment will, quite rightly, be influenced by this generalization.

The reader, as well as the writer, of history, is a chronic generalizer, applying the observation of the historian to other historical contexts with which he is familiar—or perhaps to his own time. When I read Carlyle's *French Revolution*, I find myself again and again generalizing his comments by applying them to my own special interest in the Russian revolution. Take for instance this on the terror:

Horrible, in lands that had known equal justice—not so unnatural in lands that had never known it.

Or, more significantly, this:

It is unfortunate, though very natural, that the history of this period has so generally been written in hysterics. Exaggeration abounds, execration, wailing; and on the whole, darkness.[5]

Or another, this time from Burckhardt on the growth of the modern state in the sixteenth century:

The more recently power has originated, the less it can remain stationary—first because those who created it have become accustomed to rapid further movement and because they are and will remain innovators *per se*; secondly, because the forces aroused or subdued by them can be employed only through further acts of violence.[6]

---

[5] *History of the French Revolution*, I, v, Ch. 9; III, i, Ch. 1.
[6] Burckhardt: *Judgments on History and Historians*, p. 34.

It is nonsense to say that generalization is foreign to history; history thrives on generalizations. As Mr. Elton neatly puts it in a volume of *The New Cambridge Modern History*, "what distinguishes the historian from the collector of historical facts is generalization"; [7] he might have added that the same thing distinguishes the natural scientist from the naturalist or collector of specimens. But do not suppose that generalization permits us to construct some vast scheme of history into which specific events must be fitted. And, since Marx is one of those who is often accused of constructing, or believing in, such a scheme, I will quote by way of summing-up a passage from one of his letters which puts the matter in its right perspective:

Events strikingly similar, but occurring in a different historical milieu, lead to completely dissimilar results. By studying each of these evolutions separately and then comparing them, it is easy to find the key to the understanding of this phenomenon; but it is never possible to arrive at this understanding by using the *passe-partout* of some historical-philosophical theory whose great virtue is to stand above history.[8]

---

[7] *The Cambridge Modern History*, II (1958), p. 20.

[8] Marx and Engels: *Works* (Russian ed.), xv, p. 378. The letter from which this passage is quoted appeared in the Russian journal *Otechestvennye Zapiski* in 1877. Professor Popper appears to associate Marx with what he calls "the central mistake of historicism," the belief that historical tendencies or trends "can be immediately derived from universal laws alone" (*The Poverty of Historicism* [London: Routledge & Kegan Paul; 1957], pp. 128–9): this is precisely what Marx denied.

History is concerned with the relation between the unique and the general. As a historian, you can no more separate them, or give precedence to one over the other, than you can separate fact and interpretation.

This is perhaps the place for a brief remark on the relations between history and sociology. Sociology at present faces two opposite dangers—the danger of becoming ultra-theoretical and the danger of becoming ultra-empirical. The first is the danger of losing itself in abstract and meaningless generalizations about society in general. Society with a big S is as misleading a fallacy as History with a big H. This danger is brought nearer by those who assign to sociology the exclusive task of generalizing from the unique events recorded by history: it has even been suggested that sociology is distinguished from history by having "laws." [9] The other danger is that foreseen by Karl Mannheim almost a generation ago, and very much present today, of a sociology "split into a series of dis-

---

[9] This appears to be the view of Professor Popper (*The Open Society*, 2nd ed. [London: Routledge & Kegan Paul; 1952], ii, p. 322). Unfortunately he gives an example of a sociological law: "Wherever the freedom of thought, and of the communication of thought, is effectively protected by legal institutions and institutions ensuring the publicity of discussion, there will be scientific progress." This was written in 1942 or 1943, and was evidently inspired by the belief that the Western democracies, in virtue of their institutional arrangements, would remain in the van of scientific progress—a belief since dispelled, or severely qualified, by developments in the Soviet Union. Far from being a law, it was not even a valid generalization.

crete technical problems of social readjustment." [1] Sociology is concerned with historical societies every one
of which is unique and moulded by specific historical
antecedents and conditions. But the attempt to avoid
generalization and interpretation by confining oneself
to so-called "technical" problems of enumeration and
analysis is merely to become the unconscious apologist
of a static society. Sociology, if it is to become a fruitful field of study, must, like history, concern itself with
the relation between the unique and the general. But
it must also become dynamic—a study not of society
at rest (for no such society exists), but of social change
and development. For the rest, I would only say that
the more sociological history becomes, and the more
historical sociology becomes, the better for both. Let
the frontier between them be kept wide open for two-
way traffic.

The question of generalization is closely connected
with my second question: the lessons of history. The
real point about generalization is that through it we
attempt to learn from history, to apply the lesson
drawn from one set of events to another set of events:
when we generalize, we are consciously or unconsciously trying to do this. Those who reject generalization and insist that history is concerned exclusively
with the unique are, logically enough, those who deny

---

[1] Karl Mannheim: *Ideology and Utopia* (London: Routledge &
Kegan Paul; 1936), p. 228.

that anything can be learned from history. But the assertion that men learn nothing from history is contradicted by a multitude of observable facts. No experience is more common. In 1919 I was present at the Paris peace conference as a junior member of the British delegation. Everyone in the delegation believed that we could learn from the lessons of the Vienna Congress, the last great European peace congress a hundred years earlier. A certain Captain Webster, then employed in the War Office, now Sir Charles Webster and an eminent historian, wrote an essay telling us what those lessons were. Two of them have remained in my memory. One was that it was dangerous, when re-drawing the map of Europe, to neglect the principle of self-determination. The other was that it was dangerous to throw secret documents into your waste-paper basket, the contents of which would certainly be bought by the secret service of some other delegation. These lessons of history were taken for gospel and influenced our behaviour. This example is recent and trivial. But it would be easy to trace in comparatively remote history the influence of the lessons of a still remoter past. Everyone knows about the impact of ancient Greece upon Rome. But I am not sure whether any historian has attempted to make a precise analysis of the lessons which the Romans learned, or believed themselves to have learned, from the history of Hellas. An examination of the lessons drawn in Western Europe in the seventeenth, eighteenth, and nineteenth centuries from Old

Testament history might yield rewarding results. The
English Puritan revolution cannot be fully understood
without it; and the conception of the chosen people
was an important factor in the rise of modern nationalism. The stamp of a classical education was heavily
imprinted in the nineteenth century on the new ruling
class in Great Britain. Grote, as I have already noted,
pointed to Athens as an exemplar for the new democracy; and I should like to see a study of the extensive
and important lessons consciously or unconsciously
imparted to British empire-builders by the history of
the Roman Empire. In my own particular field, the
makers of the Russian revolution were profoundly impressed—one might almost say, obsessed—by the lessons of the French revolution, of the revolutions of
1848, and of the Paris commune of 1871. But I shall
recall here the qualification imposed by the dual character of history. Learning from history is never simply
a one-way process. To learn about the present in the
 light of the past means also to learn about the past in
the light of the present. The function of history is to
promote a profounder understanding of both past and
present through the interrelation between them.

My third point is the role of prediction in history:
no lessons, it is said, can be learned from history because history, unlike science, cannot predict the future. This question is involved in a tissue of misun-
derstandings. As we have seen, scientists are no longer

so eager as they used to be to talk about the laws of nature. The so-called laws of science which affect our ordinary life are in fact statements of tendency, statements of what will happen, other things being equal, or in laboratory conditions. They do not claim to predict what will happen in concrete cases. The law of gravity does not prove that that particular apple will fall to the ground: somebody may catch it in a basket. The law of optics that light travels in a straight line does not prove that a particular ray of light may not be refracted or scattered by some intervening object. But this does not mean that these laws are worthless, or not in principle valid. Modern physical theories, we are told, deal only with the probabilities of events taking place. Today science is more inclined to remember that induction can logically lead only to probabilities or to reasonable belief, and is more anxious to treat its pronouncements as general rules or guides, the validity of which can be tested only in specific action. *"Science, d'où prévoyance; prévoyance, d'où action,"* as Comte put it.[2] The clue to the question of prediction in history lies in this distinction between the general and the specific, between the universal and the unique. The historian, as we have seen, is bound to generalize; and, in so doing, he provides √ general guides for future action which, though not specific predictions, are both valid and useful. But he cannot predict specific events, because the specific is

[2] *Cours de philosophie positive,* i, p. 51.

unique and because the element of accident enters
into it. This distinction, which worries philosophers,
is perfectly clear to the ordinary man. If two or three
children in a school develop measles, you will con-
clude that the epidemic will spread; and this prediction, if you care to call it such, is based on a generalization from past experience, and is a valid and useful
guide to action. But you cannot make the specific prediction that Charles or Mary will catch measles. The
historian proceeds in the same way. People do not
expect the historian to predict that revolution will
break out in Ruritania next month. The kind of conclusion which they will seek to draw, partly from specific knowledge of Ruritanian affairs and partly from
a study of history, is that conditions in Ruritania are
such that a revolution is likely to occur in the near
future if somebody touches it off, or unless somebody
on the government side does something to stop it; and
this conclusion might be accompanied by estimates,
based partly on the analogy of other revolutions, of
the attitude which different sectors of the population
may be expected to adopt. The prediction, if such it
can be called, can be realized only through the occurrence of unique events, which cannot themselves be
predicted. But this does not mean that inferences
drawn from history about the future are worthless, or
that they do not possess a conditional validity which
serves both as a guide to action and a key to our understanding of how things happen. I do not wish to suggest that the inferences of the social scientist or of the

historian can match those of the physical scientist in precision, or that their inferiority in this respect is due merely to the greater backwardness of the social sciences. The human being is on any view the most complex rational entity known to us, and the study of his behaviour may well involve difficulties different in kind from those confronting the physical scientist. All I wish to establish is that their aims and methods are not fundamentally dissimilar.

My fourth point introduces a far more cogent argument for drawing a line of demarcation between the social sciences, including history, and the physical sciences. This is the argument that in the social sciences subject and object belong to the same category and interact reciprocally on each other. Human beings are not only the most complex and variable of natural entities, but they have to be studied by other human beings, not by independent observers of another species. Here man is no longer content, as in the biological sciences, to study his own physical make-up and physical reactions. The sociologist, the economist, or the historian needs to penetrate into forms of human behaviour in which the will is active, to ascertain why the human beings who are the object of his study willed to act as they did. This sets up a relation, which is peculiar to history and the social sciences, between the observer and what is observed. The point of view of the historian enters irrevocably into every observation which he makes; history is shot through and through with relativity. In Karl Mannheim's words, "even the categories in which experiences are subsumed, collected, and ordered vary according to the social position of the observer." [3] But it is not merely true that the bias of the social scientist necessarily enters into all his observations. It is also true that the process of observation affects and modifies what is being observed. And this can happen in two opposite ways. The human beings whose behaviour is made the object of analysis and prediction may be warned in advance by the prediction of consequences unwelcome to them, and be induced by it to modify their action, so that the prediction, however correctly based on the analysis, proves self-frustrating. One reason why history rarely repeats itself among historically conscious people is that the *dramatis personae* are aware at the second performance of the *dénouement* of the first, and their action is affected by that knowledge. [4] The Bolsheviks knew that the French revolution had ended in a Napoleon, and feared that their own revolution might end in the same way. They therefore mistrusted Trotsky, who among their leaders looked most like a Napoleon, and trusted Stalin, who looked least like a Napoleon. But this process may work in a converse direction. The economist who, by a scientific analysis

---

[3] Mannheim: *Ideology and Utopia*, p. 130.

[4] This argument has been developed by the author in *The Bolshevik Revolution, 1917–1923* (London: Macmillan & Co.; 1950), I, p. 42.

of existing economic conditions, predicts an approaching boom or slump may, if his authority is great and his arguments cogent, contribute by the very fact of his prediction to the occurrence of the phenomenon predicted. The political scientist who, on the strength of historical observations, nourishes the conviction that despotism is short-lived, may contribute to the downfall of the despot. Everyone is familiar with the behaviour of candidates at elections who predict their own victory for the conscious purpose of rendering the fulfilment of the prediction more likely; and one suspects that economists, political scientists, and historians, when they venture on prediction, are sometimes inspired by the unconscious hope of hastening the realization of the prediction. All that one can perhaps safely say about these complex relations is that interaction between the observer and what is observed, between the social scientist and his data, between the historian and his facts, is continuous, and continuously varies; and that this appears to be a distinctive feature of history and of the social sciences.

I should perhaps note here that some physicists in recent years have spoken of their science in terms which appear to suggest more striking analogies between the physical universe and the world of the historian. In the first place, their results are said to involve a principle of uncertainty or indeterminacy. I shall speak in my next lecture of the nature and limits of so-called determinism in history. But whether the indeterminacy of modern physics resides in the nature

of the universe or is merely an index of our own hitherto imperfect understanding of it (this point is still
in debate), I should have the same doubts about finding in it significant analogies with our ability to make
historical predictions as one had a few years ago about
the attempts of some enthusiasts to find proof in it of
the operation of free will in the universe. Secondly, we
are told that in modern physics distances in space and
lapses of time have measures depending on the motion of the "observer." In modern physics all measure-
ments are subject to inherent variations due to the
impossibility of establishing a constant relation between the "observer" and the object under observation; both the "observer" and the thing observed—
both subject and object—enter into the final result of
the observation. But, while these descriptions would
apply with a minimum of change to the relations between the historian and the objects of his observations,
I am not satisfied that the essence of these relations is
in any real sense comparable with the nature of relations between the physicist and his universe; and
though I am in principle concerned to reduce rather
than to inflate the differences which separate the approach of the historian from that of the scientist, it
will not help to attempt to spirit these differences
away by relying on imperfect analogies.

But, while it is, I think, fair to say that the involvement of the social scientist or historian in the object
of his study is of a different kind than that of the
physical scientist, and the issues raised by the relation

between subject and object infinitely more complicated, this is not the end of the matter. Classical theories of knowledge, which prevailed throughout the
seventeenth, eighteenth, and nineteenth centuries, all
assumed a sharp dichotomy between the knowing subject and the object known. However the process was
conceived, the model constructed by the philosophers
showed subject and object, man and the external
world, divided and apart. This was the great age of the
birth and development of science; and theories of
knowledge were strongly influenced by the outlook of
the pioneers of science. Man was set sharply against
the external world. He grappled with it as with something intractable and potentially hostile—intractible
because it was difficult to understand, potentially hostile because it was difficult to master. With the successes of modern science this outlook has been radically modified. The scientist nowadays is far less likely
to think of the forces of nature as something to fight
against than as something to co-operate with and to
harness to his purposes. Classical theories of knowledge no longer fit the newer science, and least of all
the science of physics. It is not surprising that during
the past fifty years philosophers have begun to call
them in question, and to recognize that the process of
knowledge, far from setting subject and object sharply
apart, involves a measure of interrelation and interdependence between them. This is, however, extremely
significant for the social sciences. In my first lecture,
I suggested that the study of history was difficult to

reconcile with the traditional empiricist theory of knowledge. I should now like to argue that the social sciences as a whole, since they involve man as both subject and object, both investigator and thing investigated, are incompatible with any theory of knowledge which pronounces a rigid divorce between subject and object. Sociology, in its attempts to establish itself as a coherent body of doctrine, has quite rightly set up a branch called the sociology of knowledge. This has, however, not yet got very far—mainly, I suspect, because it has been content to go round and round inside the cage of traditional theory of knowledge. If philosophers, under the impact first of modern physical science, and now of modern social science, are beginning to break out from this cage, and construct some more up-to-date model for the processes of knowledge than the old billiard-ball model of the impact of data on a passive consciousness, this is a good omen for the social sciences and for history in particular. This is a point of some importance to which I shall return later when I come to consider what we mean by objectivity in history.

Last but not least, I have to discuss the view that history, being intimately involved in questions of religion and morality, is thereby distinguished from science in general, and perhaps even from the other social sciences. Of the relation of history to religion I shall say only the little that is necessary to make my own position clear. To be a serious astronomer is compatible with belief in a God who created and ordered the universe. But it is not compatible with belief in a God who intervenes at will to change the course of a planet, to postpone an eclipse, or to alter the rules of the cosmic game. In the same way, it is sometimes suggested, a serious historian may believe in a God who has ordered, and given meaning to, the course of history as a whole, though he cannot believe in the Old Testament kind of God who intervenes to slaughter the Amalekites, or cheats on the calendar by extending the hours of daylight for the benefit of Joshua's army. Nor can he invoke God as an explanation of particular historical events. Father D'Arcy in a recent book attempted to make this distinction:

> It would not do for a student to answer every question in history by saying that it was the finger of God. Not until we have gone as far as most in tidying up mundane events and the human drama are we permitted to bring in wider considerations.[5]

The awkwardness of this view is that it appears to treat religion like the joker in the pack of cards, to be reserved for really important tricks that cannot be taken in any other way. Karl Barth, the Lutheran theologian, did better when he pronounced a total

---

[5] M. C. D'Arcy: *The Sense of History: Secular and Sacred* (London: Faber & Faber; 1959), p. 164. He had been anticipated by Polybius: "Wherever it is possible to find out the cause of what is happening one should not have recourse to the gods" (quoted in Kurt von Fritz: *The Theory of the Mixed Constitution in Antiquity* [New York: Columbia University Press; 1954], p. 390).

separation between divine and secular history, and handed over the latter to the secular arm. Professor Butterfield, if I understand him, means the same thing when he speaks of "technical" history. Technical history is the only kind of history you or I are ever likely to write, or he himself has ever written. But by the use of this odd epithet, he reserves the right to believe in an esoteric or providential history with which the rest of us need not concern ourselves. Writers like Berdyaev, Niebuhr, and Maritain purport to maintain the autonomous status of history, but insist that the end or goal of history lies outside history. Personally, I find it hard to reconcile the integrity of history with belief in some super-historical force on which its meaning and significance depend—whether that force be the God of a Chosen People, a Christian God, the Hidden Hand of the Deist, or Hegel's World Spirit. For the purposes of these lectures, I shall assume that the historian must solve his problems without recourse to any such *deus ex machina*, that history is a game played, so to speak, without a joker in the pack.

The relation of history to morality is more complicated and discussions of it in the past have suffered from several ambiguities. It is scarcely necessary today to argue that the historian is not required to pass moral judgments on the private life of the characters in his story. The standpoints of the historian and of the moralist are not identical. Henry VIII may have been a bad husband and a good king. But the historian is interested in him in the former capacity only in so far as it affected historical events. If his moral delinquencies had had as little apparent effect on public affairs as those of Henry II, the historian would not need to bother about them. This goes for virtues as well as vices. Pasteur and Einstein were, one is told, men of exemplary, even saintly, private lives. But, suppose they had been unfaithful husbands, cruel fathers, and unscrupulous colleagues, would their historical achievements have been any the less? And it is these which preoccupy the historian. Stalin is said to have behaved cruelly and callously to his second wife; but, as a historian of Soviet affairs, I do not feel myself much concerned. This does not mean that private morality is not important, or that the history of morals is not a legitimate part of history. But the historian does not turn aside to pronounce moral judgments on the private lives of individuals who appear in his pages. He has other things to do.

The more serious ambiguity arises over the question of moral judgments on public actions. Belief in the duty of the historian to pronounce moral judgments on his *dramatis personae* has a long pedigree. But it was never more powerful than in nineteenth-century Britain, when it was reinforced both by the moralizing tendencies of the age and by the uninhibited cult of individualism. Rosebery remarked that what English people wanted to know about Napoleon was whether he was "a good man." [6] Acton in his correspondence

---

[6] Rosebery: *Napoleon: The Last Phase*, p. 364.

with Creighton declared that "the inflexibility of the moral code is the secret of the authority, the dignity, and the utility of History," and claimed to make history "an arbiter of controversy, a guide of the wanderer, the upholder of that moral standard which the powers of earth and of religion itself tend constantly to depress" [7]—a view based on Acton's almost mystical belief in the objectivity and supremacy of historical facts, which apparently requires and entitles the historian, in the name of History as a sort of super-historical power, to pass moral judgments on individuals participating in historical events. This attitude still sometimes reappears in unexpected forms. Professor Toynbee described Mussolini's invasion of Abyssinia in 1935 as a "deliberate personal sin"; [8] and Sir Isaiah Berlin in the essay already quoted insists with great vehemence that it is the duty of the historian "to judge Charlemagne or Napoleon or Genghis Khan or Hitler or Stalin for their massacres." [9] This view has

---

[7] Acton: *Historical Essays and Studies* (London: Macmillan & Co.; 1907), p. 505.

[8] *Survey of International Affairs* (London: Oxford University Press; 1935), Vol. II, p. 3.

[9] Berlin: *Historical Inevitability*, pp. 76–7. Sir Isaiah's attitude echoes the views of that sturdy nineteenth-century conservative jurist Fitzjames Stephen: "The criminal law thus proceeds upon the principle that it is morally right to hate criminals. . . . It is highly desirable that criminals should be hated, that the punishments inflicted on them should be so contrived as to give expression to that hatred, and to justify it so far as the public provision of means for expressing and gratifying a healthy natural sentiment can justify and encourage it" (A *History of the Criminal Law of England* [1883],

been sufficiently castigated by Professor Knowles, who in his inaugural lecture quoted Motley's denunciation of Philip II ("if there are vices . . . from which he was exempt, it is because it is not permitted by human nature to attain perfection even in evil"), and Stubbs's description of King John ("polluted with every crime that could disgrace a man"), as instances of moral judgments on individuals which it is not within the competence of the historian to pronounce: "The historian is not a judge, still less a hanging judge." [1] But Croce also has a fine passage on this point, which I should like to quote:

The accusation forgets the great difference that our tribunals (whether juridical or moral) are present-day tribunals designed for living, active, and dangerous men, while those other men have already appeared before the tribunal of their day, and cannot be condemned or absolved twice. They cannot be held responsible before any tribunal whatsoever, just because they are men of the past who belong to the peace of the past and as such can only be subjects of history, and can suffer no other judgment than that which penetrates and understands the spirit of their work. . . . Those who on the plea of narrating history bustle about as judges, condemning here and giving

ii, 81–2, quoted in L. Radzinowicz: *Sir James Fitzjames Stephen* [London: Macmillan & Co.; 1957], p. 30). These views are no longer widely shared by criminologists; but my quarrel with them here is that, whatever their validity elsewhere, they are not applicable to the verdicts of history.

[1] D. Knowles: *The Historian and Character* (Cambridge University Press; 1955), pp. 4–5, 12, 19.

absolution there, because they think that this is the office of history . . . are generally recognized as devoid of historical sense.[2]

And if anyone cavils at the statement that it is not our business to pass moral judgment on Hitler or Stalin— or, if you like, on Senator McCarthy—this is because they were the contemporaries of many of us, because hundreds of thousands of those who suffered directly or indirectly from their actions are still alive, and because, precisely for these reasons, it is difficult for us to approach them as historians and to divest ourselves of other capacities which might justify us in passing judgment on their deeds: this is one of the embarrassments—I should say, the principal embarrassment— of the contemporary historian. But what profit does anyone find today in denouncing the sins of Charlemagne or of Napoleon?

Let us therefore reject the notion of the historian as a hanging judge, and turn to the more difficult but more profitable question of the passing of moral judgments not on individuals, but on events, institutions, or policies of the past. These are the important judgments of the historian; and those who insist so fervently on the moral condemnation of the individual sometimes unconsciously provide an alibi for whole groups and societies. The French historian Lefebvre, seeking to exonerate the French revolution from responsibility for the disasters and bloodshed of the Na-

---

[2] B. Croce: *History as the Story of Liberty*, p. 47.

poleonic wars, attributed them to "the dictatorship of a general . . . whose temperament . . . could not easily acquiesce in peace and moderation." [3] Germans today welcome the denunciation of Hitler's individual wickedness as a satisfactory alternative to the moral judgment of the historian on the society which produced him. Russians, Englishmen, and Americans readily join in personal attacks on Stalin, Neville Chamberlain, or McCarthy as scapegoats for their collective misdeeds. Moreover, laudatory moral judgments on individuals can be just as misleading and mischievous as the moral denunciation of individuals. Recognition that some individual slave-owners were high-minded was constantly used as an excuse for not condemning slavery as immoral. Max Weber refers to "the masterless slavery in which capitalism enmeshes the worker or the debtor," and rightly argues that the historian should pass moral judgment on the institution, but not on the individuals who created it. [4] The historian does not sit in judgment on an individual oriental despot. But he is not required to remain indifferent and impartial between, say, oriental despotism and the institutions of Periclean Athens. He will not pass judgment on the individual slave-owner. But this does not prevent him from condemning a slave-owning society. Historical facts, as we saw, presuppose some measure of interpretation; and historical inter-

---

[3] *Peuples et civilisations*, XIV: *Napoléon*, p. 58.
[4] Quoted in *From Max Weber: Essays in Sociology* (London: Routledge & Kegan Paul; 1947), p. 58.

pretations always involve moral judgments—or, if you prefer a more neutral-sounding term, value judgments.

This is, however, only the beginning of our difficulties. History is a process of struggle in which results, whether we judge them good or bad, are achieved by some groups directly or indirectly—and more often directly than indirectly—at the expense of others. The losers pay. Suffering is indigenous in history. Every great period of history has its casualties as well as its victories. This is an exceedingly complicated question because we have no measure which enables us to balance the greater good of some against the sacrifices of others: yet some such balance must be struck. It is not exclusively a problem of history. In ordinary life we are more often involved than we sometimes care to admit in the necessity of preferring the lesser evil, or of doing evil that good may come. In history the question is sometimes discussed under the rubric "the cost of progress" or "the price of revolution." This is misleading. As Bacon says in the essay *On Innovations,* "the forward retention of custom is as turbulent a thing as an innovation." The cost of conservation falls just as heavily on the under-privileged as the cost of innovation on those who are deprived of their privileges. The thesis that the good of some justifies the sufferings of others is implicit in all government, and is just as much a conservative as a radical doctrine. Dr. Johnson robustly invoked the argument of the lesser evil to justify the maintenance of existing inequalities:

It is better that some should be unhappy than that none should be happy, which would be the case in a general state of equality.[5]

But it is in periods of radical change that the issue appears in its most dramatic form; and it is here that we find it easiest to study the attitude of the historian towards it.

Let us take the story of the industrialization of Great Britain between, say, about 1780 and 1870. Virtually every historian will treat the industrial revolution, probably without discussion, as a great and progressive achievement. He will also describe the driving of the peasantry off the land, the herding of workers in unhealthy factories and unsanitary dwellings, the exploitation of child labour. He will probably say that abuses occurred in the working of the system, and that some employers were more ruthless than others, and will dwell with some unction on the gradual growth of a humanitarian conscience once the system has become established. But he will assume, again probably without saying it, that measures of coercion and exploitation, at any rate in the first stages, were an unavoidable part of the cost of industrialization. Nor

---

[5] Boswell: *Life of Doctor Johnson*, 1791 (Everyman ed. ii, 20). This has the merit of candour; Burckhardt (*Judgments on History and Historians*, p. 85) sheds tears over the "silenced moans" of the victims of progress, "who, as a rule, had wanted nothing else but *parta tueri*," but is himself silent about the moans of the victims of the *ancien régime* who, as a rule, had nothing to preserve.

have I ever heard of a historian who said that, in view
of the cost, it would have been better to stay the hand
of progress and not industrialize; if any such exists, he
doubtless belongs to the school of Chesterton and
Belloc, and will—quite properly—not be taken seriously by serious historians. This example is of particular interest to me, because I hope soon in my history
of Soviet Russia to approach the problem of the col-
lectivization of the peasant as a part of the cost of industrialization; and I know well that if, following the
example of historians of the British industrial revolution, I deplore the brutalities and abuses of collectivi-
zation, but treat the process as an unavoidable part of
the cost of a desirable and necessary policy of industrialization, I shall incur charges of cynicism and of
condoning evil things. Historians condone the nineteenth-century colonization of Asia and Africa by the
Western nations on the ground not only of its immediate effects on the world economy, but of its long-
term consequences for the backward peoples of these
continents. After all, it is said, modern India is the
child of British rule; and modern China is the product
of nineteenth-century Western imperialism, crossed
with the influence of the Russian revolution. Unfortunately it was not the Chinese workers who laboured
in the Western-owned factories in the treaty ports, or
in the South African mines, or on the Western
front in the First World War, who have survived to
enjoy whatever glory or profit may have accrued from
the Chinese revolution. Those who pay the cost are

rarely those who reap the benefits. The well-known purple passage from Engels is uncomfortably apt:

History is about the most cruel of all goddesses, and she leads her triumphal car over heaps of corpses, not only in war, but also in "peaceful" economic development. And we men and women are unfortunately so stupid that we never pluck up courage for real progress unless urged to it by sufferings that seem almost out of proportion.[6]

Ivan Karamazov's famous gesture of defiance is a heroic fallacy. We are born into society, we are born into history. No moment occurs when we are offered a ticket of admission with the option to accept or reject it. The historian has no more conclusive answer than the theologian to the problem of suffering. He, too, falls back on the thesis of the lesser evil and the greater good.

But does not the fact that the historian, unlike the scientist, becomes involved by the nature of his material in these issues of moral judgment imply the submission of history to a super-historical standard of value? I do not think that it does. Let us assume that abstract conceptions like "good" and "bad," and more sophisticated developments of them, lie beyond the confines of history. But, even so, these abstractions play in the study of historical morality much the same role as mathematical and logical formulas in physical science. They are indispensable categories of thought;

---

[6] Letter of February 24, 1893, to Danielson in *Karl Marx and Friedrich Engels: Correspondence 1846–1895* (London: Lawrence & Wishart; 1934), p. 510.

but they are devoid of meaning or application till specific content is put into them. If you prefer a different metaphor, the moral precepts which we apply in history or in everyday life are like cheques on a bank: they have a printed and a written part. The printed part consists of abstract words like liberty and equality, justice and democracy. These are essential categories. But the cheque is valueless until we fill in the other part, which states how much liberty we propose to allocate to whom, whom we recognize as our equals, and up to what amount. The way in which we fill in the cheque from time to time is a matter of history. The process by which specific historical content is given to abstract moral conceptions is a historical process; indeed, our moral judgments are made within a conceptual framework which is itself the creation of history. The favourite form of contemporary international controversy on moral issues is a debate on rival claims to freedom and democracy. The conceptions are abstract and universal. But the content put into them has varied throughout history, from time to time and from place to place; any practical issue of their application can be understood and debated only in historical terms. To take a slightly less popular example, the attempt has been made to use the conception of "economic rationality" as an objective and non-controversial criterion by which the desirability of economic policies can be tested and judged. The attempt at once breaks down. Theorists brought up on the laws of classical economics condemn planning in

principle as an irrational intrusion into rational economic processes; for example, planners refuse in their
price policy to be bound by the law of supply and demand, and prices under planning can have no rational
basis. It may, of course, be true that planners often
behave irrationally, and therefore foolishly. But the
criterion by which they must be judged is not the old
"economic rationality" of classical economy. Personally, I have more sympathy with the converse argument that it was the uncontrolled, unorganized *laissez-
faire* economy which was essentially irrational, and
that planning is an attempt to introduce "economic
rationality" into the process. But the only point which
I wish to make at the moment is the impossibility of
erecting an abstract and super-historical standard by
which historical actions can be judged. Both sides inevitably read into such a standard the specific content
appropriate to their own historical conditions and aspirations.

This is the real indictment of those who seek to
erect a super-historical standard or criterion in the
light of which judgment is passed on historical events
or situations—whether that standard derives from
some divine authority postulated by the theologians,
and from a static reason or nature postulated by the
philosophers of the Enlightenment. It is not that
shortcomings occur in the application of the standard,
or defects in the standard itself. It is that the attempt
to erect such a standard is unhistorical and contradicts
the very essence of history. It provides a dogmatic

answer to questions which the historian is bound by
his vocation incessantly to ask: the historian who ac-
cepts answers in advance to these questions goes to
work with his eyes blindfolded, and renounces his vocation. History is movement; and movement implies
comparison. That is why historians tend to express
their moral judgments in words of a comparative nature like "progressive" and "reactionary" rather than
in uncompromising absolutes like "good" and "bad";
these are attempts to define different societies or historical phenomena not in relation to some absolute
standard, but in their relation to one another. Moreover, when we examine these supposedly absolute and
extra-historical values, we find that they too are in fact
rooted to history. The emergence of a particular value
or ideal at a given time or place is explained by historical conditions of place and time. The practical
content of hypothetical absolutes like equality, liberty,
justice, or natural law varies from period to period, or
from continent to continent. Every group has its own
values which are rooted in history. Every group pro-
tects itself against the intrusion of alien and incon-
venient values, which it brands by opprobrious epi-
thets as bourgeois and capitalist, or undemocratic and
totalitarian, or, more crudely still, as un-English and
un-American. The abstract standard or value, divorced
from society and divorced from history, is as much an
illusion as the abstract individual. The serious historian is the one who recognizes the historically conditioned character of all values, not the one who claims

for his own values an objectivity beyond history. The beliefs which we hold and the standards of judgment which we set up are part of history, and are as much subject to historical investigation as any other aspect of human behaviour. Few sciences today—least of all, the social sciences—would lay claim to total independence. But history has no fundamental dependence on something outside itself which would differentiate it from any other science.

Let me sum up what I have tried to say about the claim of history to be included among the sciences. The word science already covers so many different branches of knowledge, employing so many different methods and techniques, that the onus seems to rest on those who seek to exclude history rather than those who seek to include it. It is significant that the arguments for exclusion come not from scientists anxious to exclude historians from their select company, but from historians and philosophers anxious to vindicate the status of history as a branch of humane letters. The dispute reflects the prejudice of the old division between the humanities and science, in which the humanities were supposed to represent the broad culture of the ruling class, and science the skills of the technicians who served it. The words "humanities" and "humane" are themselves in this context a survival of this time-honoured prejudice; and the fact that the antithesis between science and history will not make sense in any language but English suggests the peculiarly insular character of the prejudice. My principal objection to the refusal to call history a science is that it justifies and perpetuates the rift between the so-called "two cultures." The rift itself is a product of this ancient prejudice, based on a class structure of English society which itself belongs to the past; and I am myself not convinced that the chasm which separates the historian from the geologist is any deeper or more unbridgeable than the chasm which separates the geologist from the physicist. But the way to mend the rift is not, in my view, to teach elementary science to historians or elementary history to scientists. This is a blind alley into which we have been led by muddled thinking. After all, scientists themselves do not behave in this way. I have never heard of engineers being advised to attend elementary classes in botany.

One remedy I would suggest is to improve the standard of our history, to make it—if I may dare to say so—more scientific, to make our demands on those who pursue it more rigorous. History as an academic discipline in this university is sometimes thought of as a catch-all for those who find classics too difficult and science too serious. One impression which I hope to convey in these lectures is that history is a far more difficult subject than classics, and quite as serious as any science. But this remedy would imply a stronger faith among historians themselves in what they are doing. Sir Charles Snow, in a recent lecture on this theme, had a point when he contrasted the "brash" optimism of the scientist with the "subdued voice" and "anti-social feeling" of what he called the "literary intellectual." [7] Some historians—and more of those who write about history without being historians—belong to this category of "literary intellectuals." They are so busy telling us that history is not a science, and explaining what it cannot and should not be or do, that they have no time for its achievements and its potentialities.

The other way to heal the rift is to promote a profounder understanding of the identity of aim between scientists and historians, and this is the main value of the new and growing interest in the history and philosophy of science. Scientists, social scientists, and historians are all engaged in different branches of the same study: the study of man and his environment, of the effects of man on his environment and of his environment on man. The object of the study is the same: to increase man's understanding of, and mastery over, his environment. The presuppositions and the methods of the physicist, the geologist, the psychologist, and the historian differ widely in detail; nor do I wish to commit myself to the proposition that, in order to be more scientific, the historian must follow more closely the methods of physical science. But historian and physical scientist are united in the funda-

---

[7] C. P. Snow: *The Two Cultures and the Scientific Revolution* (London: Macmillan & Co.; 1959), pp. 4–8.

mental purpose of seeking to explain, and in the fundamental procedure of question and answer. The historian, like any other scientist, is an animal who incessantly asks the question: Why? In my next lecture I shall examine the ways in which he puts the question and in which he attempts to answer it.

CHAPTER IV

CAUSATION IN HISTORY

IF MILK is set to boil in a saucepan, it boils over. I do not know, and have never wanted to know, why this happens; if pressed, I should probably attribute it to a propensity in milk to boil over, which is true enough but explains nothing. But then I am not a natural scientist. In the same way, one can read, or even write, about the events of the past without wanting to know why they happened, or be content to say that the Second World War occurred because Hitler wanted war, which is true enough but explains nothing. But one should not then commit the solecism of calling oneself a student of history or a historian. The study of history is a study of causes. The historian, as I said at the end of my last lecture, continuously asks the question: Why?; and, so long as he hopes for an answer, he cannot rest. The great historian—or perhaps I should say more broadly, the great thinker—is the man who asks the question: Why?, about new things or in new contexts.

Herodotus, the father of history, defined his purpose in the opening of his work: to preserve a memory of the deeds of the Greeks and the barbarians, "and in particular, beyond everything else, to give the cause of their fighting one another." He found few disciples

in the ancient world: even Thucydides has been accused of having no clear conception of causation.[1] But
when in the eighteenth century the foundations of
modern historiography began to be laid, Montesquieu,
in his *Considerations on the Causes of the Greatness
of the Romans and of Their Rise and Decline*, took as
his starting-point the principles that "there are general
causes, moral or physical, which operate in every monarchy, raise it, maintain it, or overthrow it," and that
"all that occurs is subject to these causes." A few years
later in *De l'esprit des lois* he developed and generalized this idea. It was absurd to suppose that "blind
fate has produced all the effects which we see in the
world." Men were "not governed uniquely by their
fantasies"; their behavior followed certain laws or
principles derived from "the nature of things."[2] For
nearly two hundred years after that, historians and philosophers of history were busily engaged in an attempt
to organize the past experience of mankind by discovering the causes of historical events and the laws which
governed them. Sometimes the causes and the laws
were thought of in mechanical, sometimes in biological, terms, sometimes as metaphysical, sometimes as
economic, sometimes as psychological. But it was accepted doctrine that history consisted in marshalling
the events of the past in an orderly sequence of cause
and effect. "If you have nothing to tell us," wrote
Voltaire in his article on history for the Encyclopedia,

---

[1] F. M. Cornford: *Thucydides Mythistoricus, passim.*
[2] *De l'esprit des lois,* Preface and Ch. 1.

"except that one barbarian succeeded another on the banks of the Oxus and Jaxartes, what is that to us?" In the last years the picture has been somewhat modified. Nowadays, for reasons discussed in my last lecture, we no longer speak of historical "laws"; and even the word "cause" has gone out of fashion, partly owing to certain philosophical ambiguities into which I need not enter, and partly owing to its supposed association with determinism, to which I will come presently. Some people therefore speak not of "cause" in history, but of "explanation" or "interpretation," or of "the logic of the situation" or of "the inner logic of events" (this comes from Dicey), or reject the causal approach (why it happened) in favour of the functional approach (how it happened), though this seems inevitably to involve the question of how it came to happen, and so leads us straight back to question why. Other people distinguish between different kinds of cause—mechanical, biological, psychological, and so forth—and regard historical cause as a category of its own. Though some of these distinctions are in some degree valid, it may be more profitable for present purposes to stress what is common to all kinds of cause, than what separates them. For myself, I shall be content to use the word "cause" in the popular sense and neglect these particular refinements.

Let us begin by asking what the historian in practice does when he is confronted by the necessity of assigning causes to events. The first characteristic of the historian's approach to the problem of cause is that he will commonly assign several causes to the same event. Marshall the economist once wrote that "people must be warned off by every possible means from consider- ing the action of any one cause . . . without taking account of the others whose effects are commingled with it." [3] The examination candidate who in answer- ing the question: "Why did revolution break out in Russia in 1917?" offered only one cause would be lucky to get a third class. The historian deals in a mul- tiplicity of causes. If he were required to consider the causes of the Bolshevik revolution, he might name Russia's successive military defeats, the collapse of the Russian economy under pressure of war, the effective propaganda of the Bolsheviks, the failure of the Tsarist government to solve the agrarian problem, the con- centration of an impoverished and exploited proletar- iat in the factories of Petrograd, the fact that Lenin knew his own mind and nobody on the other side did —in short, a random jumble of economic, political, ideological, and personal causes, of long-term and short-term causes.

But this brings us at once to the second characteris- tic of the historian's approach. The candidate who in reply to our question was content to set out one after the other a dozen causes of the Russian revolution and leave it at that might get a second class, but scarcely a first; "well-informed, but unimaginative" would proba- bly be the verdict of the examiners. The true historian,

---

[3] *Memorials of Alfred Marshall*, ed. A. C. Pigou (London: Mac- millan & Co.; 1925), p. 428.

confronted with this list of causes of his own compil-
ing, would feel a professional compulsion to reduce it
to order, to establish some hierarchy of causes which
would fix their relation to one another, perhaps to
decide which cause, or which category of causes,
should be regarded "in the last resort" or "in the final
analysis" (favourite phrases of historians) as the ultimate cause, the cause of all causes. This is his interpretation of his theme; the historian is known by the
causes which he invokes. Gibbon attributed the decline and fall of the Roman Empire to the triumph of
barbarism and religion. The English Whig historians
of the nineteenth century attributed the rise of British
power and prosperity to the development of political
institutions embodying the principles of constitutional
liberty. Gibbon and the English nineteenth-century
historians have an old-fashioned look today because
they ignore the economic causes which modern historians have moved into the forefront. Every historical
argument revolves around the question of the priority
of causes.

Henri Poincaré, in the work which I quoted in my
last lecture, noted that science was advancing simultaneously "towards variety and complexity" and "towards unity and simplicity," and that this dual and
apparently contradictory process was a necessary condition of knowledge.[4] This is no less true of history.
The historian, by expanding and deepening his re-

---

[4] Henri Poincaré: *La Science et l'hypothèse* (1902), pp. 202–3.

search, constantly accumulates more and more answers to the question: Why? The proliferation in recent years of economic, social, cultural, and legal history—not to mention fresh insights into the complexities of political history, and the new techniques of psychology and statistics—have enormously increased the number and range of our answers. When Bertrand Russell observed that "every advance in a science takes us further away from the crude uniformities which are first observed into a greater differentiation of antecedent and consequent and into a continually wider circle of antecedents recognized as relevant," [5] he accurately described the situation in history. But the historian, in virtue of his urge to understand the past, is simultaneously compelled, like the scientist, to simplify the multiplicity of his answers, to subordinate one answer to another, and to introduce some order and unity into the chaos of happenings and the chaos of specific causes. "One God, one Law, one Element, and one far-off divine event," or Henry Adams's quest for "some great generalization which would finish one's clamour to be educated" [6]—these read nowadays like old-fashioned jokes. But the fact remains that the historian must work through the simplification, as well as through the multiplication, of causes. History, like

---

[5] Bertrand Russell: *Mysticism and Logic* (London: Longmans, Green & Co.; 1918), p. 188.

[6] *The Education of Henry Adams* (Boston: Houghton Mifflin Company; 1928), p. 224.

science, advances through this dual and apparently contradictory process.

At this point I must reluctantly turn aside to deal with two savoury red herrings which have been drawn across our path—one labelled "Determinism in History, or the Wickedness of Hegel"; the other, "Chance in History, or Cleopatra's Nose." First I must say a word or two about how they come to be here. Professor Karl Popper, who in the 1930's in Vienna wrote a weighty work on the new look in science, recently translated into English under the title *The Logic of Scientific Enquiry*, published in English during the war two books of a more popular character: *The Open Society and Its Enemies* and *The Poverty of Historicism*.[7] They were written under the strong emotional influence of the reaction against Hegel, who was treated, together with Plato, as the spiritual ancestor of Nazism, and against the rather shallow Marxism which was the intellectual climate of the British Left in the 1930's. The principal targets were the allegedly determinist philosophies of history of Hegel and Marx, grouped together under the opprobrious name of "historicism."[8] In 1954 Sir Isaiah Berlin published his

---

[7] *The Poverty of Historicism* was first published in book form in 1957, but consists of articles originally published in 1944 and 1945.

[8] I have avoided the word "historicism" except in one or two places where precision was not required, since Professor Popper's widely read writings on the subject have emptied the term of precise meaning. Constant insistence on the definition of terms is pedantic. But one must know what one is talking about, and Professor Popper

essay on *Historical Inevitability*. He dropped the attack on Plato, perhaps out of some lingering respect
for that ancient pillar of the Oxford Establishment; [9]
and he added to the indictment the argument, not
found in Popper, that the "historicism" of Hegel and
Marx is objectionable because, by explaining human
actions in causal terms, it implies a denial of human
free will, and encourages historians to evade their supposed obligation, of which I spoke in my last lecture,
to pronounce moral condemnation on the Charle-
magnes, Napoleons, and Stalins of history. Otherwise,
not much has changed. But Sir Isaiah Berlin is a de-
servedly popular and widely read writer. During the
past five or six years, almost everyone in this country or

---

uses "historicism" as a catch-all for any opinion about history
which he dislikes, including some which seem to me sound and
others which are, I suspect, held by no serious writer today. As he
admits (*The Poverty of Historicism*, p. 3), he invents "historicist"
arguments which have never been used by any known "historicist."
In his writing, historicism covers both doctrines which assimilate
history to science, and doctrines which sharply differentiate the
two. In *The Open Society*, Hegel, who rejected prediction, is
treated as the high-priest of historicism; in the introduction to
The Poverty of Historicism, historicism is described as "an approach
to the social sciences which assumes that *historical prediction* is their
principal aim." Hitherto "historicism" has been commonly used as
the English version of the German "Historismus"; now Professor
Popper distinguishes "historicism" from "historism," thus adding a
further element of confusion to the already confused usage of the
term. M. C. D'Arcy: *The Sense of History: Secular and Sacred*,
p. 11, uses the word "historicism" as "identical with a philosophy
of history."

⁹ The attack on Plato as the first Fascist originated, however, in
a series of broadcasts by an Oxford man, R. H. Crossman: *Plato
Today* (London: George Allen & Unwin; 1937).

in the United States who has written an article about
history, or even a serious review of a historical work,
has cocked a knowing snook at Hegel and Marx and
determination, and pointed out the absurdity of failing
to recognize the role of accident in history. It is perhaps unfair to hold Sir Isaiah responsible for his disciples. Even when he talks nonsense, he earns our in-
dulgence by talking it in an engaging and attractive
way. The disciples repeat the nonsense, and fail to
make it attractive. In any case, there is nothing new in
all this. Charles Kingsley, not the most distinguished
of our Regius Professors of Modern History, who had
probably never read Hegel or heard of Marx, spoke
in his inaugural lecture in 1860 of man's "mysterious
power of breaking the laws of his own being" as proof
that no "inevitable sequence" could exist in history.[1]
But fortunately we had forgotten Kingsley. It is Professor Popper and Sir Isaiah Berlin who between them
have flogged this very dead horse back into a sem-
blance of life; and some patience will be required to
clear up the muddle.

First, then, let me take determinism, which I will
define—I hope, uncontroversially—as the belief that
everything that happens has a cause or causes, and
could not have happened differently unless something

---

[1] C. Kingsley: *The Limits of Exact Science as Applied to History*
(1860), p. 22.

in the cause or causes had also been different.[2] Determinism is a problem not of history, but of all human behaviour. The human being whose actions have no cause and are therefore undetermined is as much an abstraction as the individual outside society whom we discussed in a previous lecture. Professor Popper's assertion that "everything is possible in human affairs" [3] is either meaningless or false. Nobody in ordinary life believes or can believe this. The axiom that everything has a cause is a condition of our capacity to understand what is going on around us.[4] The nightmare quality of Kafka's novels lies in the fact that nothing that happens has any apparent cause, or any cause that can be ascertained: this leads to the total disintegration of the human personality, which is based on the assumption that events have causes, and that enough of these causes are ascertainable to build up in the human mind a pattern of past and present sufficiently coherent to serve as a guide to action. Everyday life would be impossible unless one assumed that

---

[2] "Determinism . . . means . . . that, the data being what they are whatever happens happens definitely and could not be different. To hold that it could, means only that it would if the data were different" (S. W. Alexander in *Essays Presented to Ernst Cassirer* [1936], p. 18).

[3] Karl R. Popper: *The Open Society*, 2nd. ed., II, p. 197.

[4] "The Law of Causality is not imposed upon us by the world," but "is perhaps for us the most convenient method of adapting ourselves to the world" (J. Rueff: *From the Physical to the Social Sciences* [Baltimore: Johns Hopkins Press; 1929], p. 52); Professor Popper himself (*The Logic of Scientific Enquiry*, p. 248) calls belief in causality a "metaphysical hypostatization of a well-justified methodological rule."

human behavior was determined by causes which are in principle ascertainable. Once upon a time some people thought it blasphemous to enquire into the causes of natural phenomena, since these were obviously governed by the divine will. Sir Isaiah Berlin's objection to our explaining why human beings acted as they did, on the ground that these actions are governed by the human will, belongs to the same order of ideas, and perhaps indicates that the social sciences are in the same stage of development today as were the natural sciences when this kind of argument was directed against them.

Let us see how we handle this problem in everyday life. As you go about your daily affairs, you are in the habit of meeting Smith. You greet him with an amiable, but pointless, remark about the weather, or about the state of college or university business; he replies with an equally amiable and pointless remark about the weather or the state of business. But supposing that one morning Smith, instead of answering your remark in his usual way, were to break into a violent diatribe against your personal appearance or character. Would you shrug your shoulders, and treat this as a convincing demonstration of the freedom of Smith's will and of the fact that everything is possible in human affairs? I suspect that you would not. On the contrary, you would probably say something like: "Poor Smith. You know, of course, that his father died in a mental hospital," or "Poor Smith! He must have been having more trouble with his wife." In other words, you would attempt to diagnose the cause of Smith's apparently causeless behaviour in the firm conviction that some cause there must be. By so doing you would, I fear, incur the wrath of Sir Isaiah Berlin, who would bitterly complain that, by providing a causal explanation of Smith's behavior, you had swallowed Hegel's and Marx's deterministic assumption, and shirked your obligation to denounce Smith as a cad. But nobody in ordinary life takes this view, or supposes that either determinism or moral responsibility is at stake. The logical dilemma about free will and determinism does not arise in real life. It is not that some human actions are free and others determined. The fact is that all human actions are both free and determined, according to the point of view from which one considers them. The practical question is different again. Smith's action had a cause, or a number of causes; but in so far as it was caused not by some external compulsion, but by the compulsion of his own personality, he was morally responsible, since it is a condition of social life that normal adult human beings are morally responsible for their own personality. Whether to hold him responsible in this particular case is a matter for your practical judgment. But, if you do, this does not mean that you regard his action as having no cause: cause and moral responsibility are different categories. An Institute and Chair of Criminology have recently been established in this university. It would not, I feel sure, occur to any of those engaged in investigating the causes of crime to suppose that this committed them to a denial of the moral responsibility of the criminal.

Now let us look at the historian. Like the ordinary man, he believes that human actions have causes which are in principle ascertainable. History, like everyday life, would be impossible if this assumption were not made. It is the special function of the historian to investigate these causes. This may be thought to give him a special interest in the determined aspect of human behaviour: but he does not reject free will —except on the untenable hypothesis that voluntary actions have no cause. Nor is he troubled by the question of inevitability. Historians, like other people, sometimes fall into rhetorical language and speak of an occurrence as "inevitable" when they mean merely that the conjunction of factors leading one to expect it was overwhelmingly strong. Recently I searched my own history for the offending word, and cannot give myself an entirely clean bill of health: in one passage I wrote that, after the revolution of 1917, a clash between the Bolsheviks and the Orthodox Church was "inevitable." No doubt it would have been wiser to say "extremely probable." But may I be excused for finding the correction a shade pedantic? In practice, historians do not assume that events are inevitable before they have taken place. They frequently discuss alternative courses available to the actors in the story on the assumption that the option was open, though they go on quite correctly to explain why one course was eventually chosen rather than the other. Nothing in history is inevitable except in the formal sense that, for it to have happened otherwise, the antecedent causes would have had to be different. As a historian, I am perfectly prepared to do without "inevitable," "unavoidable," "inescapable," and even "ineluctable." Life will be drabber. But let us leave them to poets and metaphysicians.

So barren and pointless does this charge of inevitability appear, and so great the vehemence with which it has been pursued in recent years, that I think we must look for the hidden motives behind it. Its principal source is, I suspect, what I may call the "might-have-been" school of thought—or rather of emotion. It attaches itself almost exclusively to contemporary history. Last term here in Cambridge I saw a talk to some society advertised under the title: "Was the Russian Revolution Inevitable?" I am sure it was intended as a perfectly serious talk. But if you had seen a talk advertised on "Were the Wars of the Roses Inevitable?" you would at once have suspected some joke. The historian writes of the Norman conquest or the American war of independence as if what happened was in fact bound to happen, and as if it was his business simply to explain what happened and why; and nobody accuses him of being a determinist and of failing to discuss the alternative possibility that William the Conqueror or the American insurgents might have been defeated. When, however, I write about the Russian revolution of 1917 in precisely this way—the only proper way to the historian—I find myself under attack from my critics for having by implication depicted what happened as something that was bound to happen, and failed to examine all the other things that might have happened. Suppose, it is said, that Stolypin had had time to complete his agrarian reform, or that Russia had not gone to war, perhaps the revolution would not have occurred; or suppose that the Kerensky government had made good, and that leadership of the revolution had been assumed by the Mensheviks or the Social Revolutionaries instead of by the Bolsheviks. These suppositions are theoretically conceivable; and one can always play a parlour game with the might-have-beens of history. But they have nothing to do with determinism; for the determinist will only reply that, for these things to have happened, the causes would also have had to be different. Nor have they anything to do with history. The point is that today nobody seriously wishes to reverse the results of the Norman conquest or of American independence or to express a passionate protest against these events; and nobody objects when the historian treats them as a closed chapter. But plenty of people, who have suffered directly or vicariously from the results of the Bolshevik victory, or still fear its remoter consequences, desire to register their protest against it; and this takes the form, when they read history, of letting their imagination run riot on all the more agreeable things that might have happened, and of being indignant with the historian who goes on quietly with his job of explaining what did happen and why their agreeable wish-dreams remain unfulfilled. The trouble about contemporary history is that people remember the time when all the options were still open, and find it difficult to adopt the attitude of the historian, for whom they have been closed by the *fait accompli*. This is a purely emotional and unhistorical reaction. But it has furnished most of the fuel for the recent campaign against the supposed doctrine of "historical inevitability." Let us get rid of this red herring once and for all.

The other source of the attack is the famous crux of Cleopatra's nose. This is the theory that history is, by and large, a chapter of accidents, a series of events determined by chance coincidences and attributable only to the most casual causes. The result of the battle of Actium was due not to the sort of causes commonly postulated by historians, but to Antony's infatuation with Cleopatra. When Bajazet was deterred by an attack of gout from marching into central Europe, Gibbon observed that "an acrimonious humour falling on a single fibre of one man may prevent or suspend the misery of nations." [5] When King Alexander of Greece died in the autumn of 1920 from the bite of a pet monkey, this accident touched off a train of events which led Sir Winston Churchill to remark that "a quarter of a million persons died of this monkey's

---

[5] Gibbon: *The Decline and Fall of the Roman Empire*, Ch. lxiv.

bite." [6] Or take again Trotsky's comment on the fever
contracted while shooting ducks which put him out of
action at a critical point of his quarrel with Zinoviev,
Kamenev, and Stalin in the autumn of 1923: "One
can foresee a revolution or a war, but it is impossible
to foresee the consequences of an autumn shooting-
trip for wild ducks." [7] The first thing to be made clear
is that this question has nothing to do with the issue
of determinism. Antony's infatuation with Cleopatra,
or Bajazet's attack of gout, or Trotsky's feverish chill,
were just as much causally determined as anything
else that happens. It is unnecessarily discourteous to
Cleopatra's beauty to suggest that Antony's infatuation had no cause. The connexion between female
beauty and male infatuation is one of the most regular
sequences of cause and effect observable in everyday
life. These so-called accidents in history represent a
sequence of cause and effect interrupting—and, so to
speak, clashing with—the sequence which the historian is primarily concerned to investigate. Bury, quite
rightly, speaks of a "collision of two independent
causal chains." [8] Sir Isaiah Berlin, who opens his essay
on *Historical Inevitability* by citing with praise an
article of Bernard Berenson on "The Accidental View
of History," is one of those who confuse accident in

---

[6] Winston Churchill: *The World Crisis: The Aftermath* (London: Butterworth & Co.; 1929), p. 386.

[7] Leon Trotsky: *My Life* (London: Butterworth & Co.; 1930),
p. 425.

[8] For Bury's argument on this point see *The Idea of Progress*
(London: Macmillan & Co.; 1920), pp. 303–4.

this sense with an absence of causal determination. But, this confusion apart, we have a real problem on our hands. How can one discover in history a coherent sequence of cause and effect, how can we find any meaning in history, when our sequence is liable to be broken or deflected at any moment by some other, and from our point of view irrelevant, sequence?

We may pause here for a moment to notice the origin of this recent widespread insistence on the role of chance in history. Polybius appears to have been the first historian to occupy himself with it in any systematic way; and Gibbon was quick to unmask the reason. "The Greeks," observed Gibbon, "after their country had been reduced to a province, imputed the triumphs of Rome not to the merit, but to the fortune, of the republic." [9] Tacitus, also a historian of the decay of his country, was another ancient historian to indulge in extensive reflexions on chance. The renewed insistence by British writers on the importance of accident in history dates from the growth of a mood of uncertainty and apprehension which set in with the present century and became marked after 1914. The first British historian to sound this note after a long

_____

[9] Gibbon: *The Decline and Fall of the Roman Empire*, Ch. 38. It is amusing to note that the Greeks, after their conquest by the Romans, also indulged in the game of historical "might-have-beens" —the favourite consolation of the defeated: if Alexander the Great had not died young, they told themselves, "he would have conquered the West and Rome would have become subject to Greek kings" (K. von Fritz: *The Theory of the Mixed Constitution in Antiquity* [New York: Columbia University Press; 1954], p. 395).

interval appears to have been Bury, who in an article
of 1909 on "Darwinism in History" drew attention to
"the element of chance coincidence" which in large
measure "helps to determine events in social evolution"; and a separate article was devoted to this theme
in 1916 under the title "Cleopatra's Nose."[1] H. A. L.
Fisher in the passage already quoted, which reflects
his disillusionment over the failure of liberal dreams
after the First World War, begs his readers to recognize "the play of the contingent and the unforeseen"
in history.[2] The popularity in this country of a theory
of history as a chapter of accidents has coincided with
the rise in France of a school of philosophers who
preach that existence—I quote Sartre's famous *L'Être
et le néant*—has "neither cause nor reason nor necessity." In Germany, the veteran historian Meinecke, as
we have already noted, became impressed towards the
end of his life with the role of chance in history. He
reproached Ranke with not having paid sufficient attention to it; and after the Second World War he at-

---

[1] Both articles are reprinted in Bury's *Selected Essays*; for Collingwood's comments on Bury's views, see *The Idea of History*, pp.
148–50.

[2] For the passage, see p. 52 above. Toynbee's quotation of Fisher's dictum in *A Study of History*, V, p. 414, reveals a complete
misapprehension: he regards it as a product of the "modern Western belief in the omnipotence of chance," which "gave birth" to
laissez-faire. The theorists of *laissez-faire* believed not in chance, but
in the hidden hand which imposed beneficent regularities on the
diversity of human behaviour; and Fisher's remark was a product
not of *laissez-faire* liberalism, but of its break-down in the 1920's
and 1930's.

tributed the national disasters of the past forty years
to a series of accidents, the vanity of the Kaiser, the
election of Hindenburg to the presidency of the Weimar Republic, Hitler's obsessional character, and so
forth—the bankruptcy of a great historian's mind under the stress of the misfortunes of his country.[3] In
a group or a nation which is riding in the trough, not
on the crest, of historical events, theories that stress
the role of chance or accident in history will be found
to prevail. The view that examination results are all
a lottery will always be popular among those who have
been placed in the third class.

But to uncover the sources of a belief is not to dispose of it; and we have still to discover exactly what
Cleopatra's nose is doing in the pages of history. Montesquieu was apparently the first who attempted to
defend the laws of history against this intrusion. "If
a particular cause, like the accidental result of a battle,
has ruined a state," he wrote in his work on the greatness and decline of the Romans, "there was a general
cause which made the downfall of this state ensue
from a single battle." The Marxists also had some difficulty over this question. Marx wrote of it only once,
and that only in a letter:

World history would have a very mystical character if
there were no room in it for chance. This chance itself
naturally becomes part of the general trend of develop-

---

[3] The relevant passages are quoted by W. Stark in his introduction
to F. Meinecke: *Machiavellism*, pp. xxxv–xxxvi.

ment and is compensated by other forms of chance. But acceleration and retardation depend on such "accidentals," which include the "chance" character of the individuals who are at the head of a movement at the outset.[4]

Marx thus offered an apology for chance in history under three heads. First, it was not very important; it could "accelerate" or "retard," but not, by implication, radically alter, the course of events. Second, one chance was compensated by another, so that in the end chance cancelled itself out. Third, chance was especially illustrated in the character of individuals.[5] Trotsky reinforced the theory of compensating and self-cancelling accidents by an ingenious analogy:

The entire historical process is a refraction of historical law through the accidental. In the language of biology, we might say that the historical law is realized through the natural selection of accidents.[6]

I confess that I find this theory unsatisfying and unconvincing. The role of accident in history is nowadays seriously exaggerated by those who are interested to stress its importance. But it exists, and to say that it merely accelerates or retards, but does not alter, is to juggle with words. Nor do I see any reason to believe

---

[4] Marx and Engels: *Works* (Russian ed.), xxvi, 108.

[5] Tolstoy in *War and Peace*, Epilogue i, equated "chance" and "genius" as terms expressive of human inability to understand ultimate causes.

[6] Leon Trotsky: *My Life*, p. 422.

that an accidental occurrence—say, the premature death of Lenin at the age of fifty-four—is automatically compensated by some other accident in such a way as to restore the balance of the historical process.

Equally inadequate is the view that accident in history is merely the measure of our ignorance—simply a name for something which we fail to understand.[7] This no doubt sometimes happens. The planets got their name, which means of course "wanderers," when they were supposed to wander at random through the sky, and the regularity of their movements was not understood. To describe something as a mischance is a favourite way of exempting oneself from the tiresome obligation to investigate its cause; and, when somebody tells me that history is a chapter of accidents, I tend to suspect him of intellectual laziness or low intellectual vitality. It is common practice with serious historians to point out that something hitherto treated as accidental was not an accident at all, but can be rationally explained and significantly fitted into the broader pattern of events. But this also does not fully answer our question. Accident is not simply something which we fail to understand. The solution of the problem of accident in history must, I believe, be sought in a quite different order of ideas.

At an earlier stage we saw that history begins with

---

[7] Tolstoy took this view: "We are forced to fall back on fatalism as an explanation of irrational events, that is to say, of events the rationality of which we do not understand" (*War and Peace*, ix, Ch. i); see also the passage cited in note 5 above.

the selection and marshalling of facts by the historian
to become historical facts. Not all facts are historical
facts. But the distinction between historical and unhistorical facts is not rigid or constant; and any fact may,
so to speak, be promoted to the status of historical fact
once its relevance and significance is discerned. We
now see that a somewhat similar process is at work in
the historian's approach to causes. The relation of the
historian to his causes has the same dual and reciprocal
character as the relation of the historian to his facts.
The causes determine his interpretation of the historical process, and his interpretation determines his selection and marshalling of the causes. The hierarchy of
causes, the relative significance of one cause or set of
causes or of another, is the essence of his interpretation. And this furnishes the clue to the problem of the
accidental in history. The shape of Cleopatra's nose,
Bajazet's attack of gout, the monkey-bite that killed
King Alexander, the death of Lenin—these were accidents which modified the course of history. It is futile to attempt to spirit them away, or to pretend that
in some way or other they had no effect. On the other
hand, in so far as they were accidental, they do not
enter into any rational interpretation of history, or into
the historian's hierarchy of significant causes. Professor Popper and Professor Berlin—I cite them once
more as the most distinguished and widely read repre-
sentatives of the school—assume that the historian's
attempt to find significance in the historical process
and to draw conclusions from it is tantamount to an

attempt to reduce "the whole of experience" to a symmetrical order, and that the presence of accident in history dooms any such attempt to failure. But no sane historian pretends to do anything so fantastic as to embrace "the whole of experience"; he cannot embrace more than a minute fraction of the facts even of his chosen sector or aspect of history. The world of the historian, like the world of the scientist, is not a photographic copy of the real world, but rather a working model which enables him more or less effectively to understand it and to master it. The historian distils from the experience of the past, or from so much of the experience of the past as is accessible to him, that part which he recognizes as amenable to rational explanation and interpretation, and from it draws conclusions which may serve as a guide to action. A recent popular writer, speaking of the achievements of science, refers graphically to the processes of the human mind which, "rummaging in the ragbag of observed 'facts,' selects, pieces, and patterns the *relevant* observed facts together, rejecting the *irrelevant*, until it has sewn together a logical and rational quilt of 'knowledge.' "[8] With some qualification as to the dangers of undue subjectivism, I should accept that as a picture of the way in which the mind of the historian works.

This procedure may puzzle and shock philosophers, and even some historians. But it is perfectly familiar

---

[8] Leslie Paul: *The Annihilation of Man* (London: Faber & Faber; 1944), p. 147.

to ordinary people going about the practical business of life. Let me illustrate. Jones, returning from a party at which he has consumed more than his usual ration of alcohol, in a car whose brakes turn out to have been defective, at a blind corner where visibility is notoriously poor, knocks down and kills Robinson, who was crossing the road to buy cigarettes at the shop on the corner. After the mess has been cleared up, we meet—say, at local police headquarters—to enquire into the causes of the occurrence. Was it due to the driver's semi-intoxicated condition—in which case there might be criminal prosecution? Or was it due to the defective brakes—in which case something might be said to the garage which overhauled the car only the week before? Or was it due to the blind corner— in which case the road authorities might be invited to give the matter their attention? While we are discussing these practical questions, two distinguished gentlemen—I shall not attempt to identify them—burst into the room and begin to tell us, with great fluency and cogency, that, if Robinson had not happened to run out of cigarettes that evening, he would not have been crossing the road and would not have been killed; that Robinson's desire for cigarettes was therefore the cause of his death; and that any enquiry which neglects this cause will be waste of time, and any conclusions drawn from it meaningless and futile. Well, what do we do? As soon as we can break into the flow of eloquence, we edge our two visitors gently but firmly towards the door, we instruct the janitor on no account to admit them again, and we get on with our enquiry. But what answer have we to the interrupters? Of course, Robinson was killed because he was a cigarette-smoker. Everything that the devotees of chance and contingency in history say is perfectly true and perfectly logical. It has the kind of remorseless logic which we find in *Alice in Wonderland* and *Through the Looking-Glass*. But, while I yield to none in my admiration for these ripe examples of Oxford scholarship, I prefer to keep my different modes of logic in separate compartments. The Dodgsonian mode is not the mode of history.

History therefore is a process of selection in terms of historical significance. To borrow Talcott Parson's phrase once more, history is "a selective system" not only of cognitive but of causal orientations to reality. Just as from the infinite ocean of facts the historian selects those which are significant for his purpose, so from the multiplicity of sequences of cause and effect he extracts those, and only those, which are historically significant; and the standard of historical significance is his ability to fit them into his pattern of rational explanation and interpretation. Other sequences of cause and effect have to be rejected as accidental, not because the relation between cause and effect is different, but because the sequence itself is irrelevant. The historian can do nothing with it; it is not amenable to rational interpretation, and has no meaning either for the past or the present. It is true that Cleopatra's nose, or Bajazet's gout, or Alexander's monkey-bite, or Lenin's death, or Robinson's cigarette-smoking, had results. But it makes no sense as a general proposition to say that generals lose battles because they are infatuated with beautiful queens, or that wars occur because kings keep pet monkeys, or that people get run over and killed on the roads because they smoke cigarettes. If, on the other hand, you tell the ordinary man that Robinson was killed because the driver was drunk, or because the brakes did not work, or because there was a blind corner on the road, this will seem to him a perfectly sensible and rational explanation; if he chooses to discriminate, he may even say that this, and not Robinson's desire for cigarettes, was the "real" cause of Robinson's death. Similarly, if you tell the student of history that the struggles in the Soviet Union in the 1920's were due to discussions about the rate of industrialization, or about the best means of inducing the peasants to grow grain to feed the towns, or even to the personal ambitions of rival leaders, he will feel that these are rational and historically significant explanations in the sense that they could also be applied to other historical situations, and that they are "real" causes of what happened in the sense that the accident of Lenin's premature death was not. He may even, if he is given to reflexion on these things, be reminded of Hegel's much quoted and much misunderstood dictum in the introduction to the *Philosophy of Right* that "what is rational is real, and what is real is rational."

Let us return for a moment to the causes of Robinson's death. We had no difficulty in recognizing that

some of the causes were rational and "real" and that
others were irrational and accidental. But by what criterion did we make the distinction? The faculty of reason is normally exercised for some purpose. Intellectuals may sometimes reason, or think that they reason,
for fun. But, broadly speaking, human beings reason
to an end. And when we recognized certain explanations as rational, and other explanations as not rational, we were, I suggest, distinguishing between explanations which served some end and explanations
which did not. In the case under discussion it made
sense to suppose that the curbing of alcoholic indul-
gence in drivers, or a stricter control over the condition of brakes, or an improvement in the siting of
roads, might serve the end of reducing the number of
traffic fatalities. But it made no sense at all to suppose
that the number of traffic fatalities could be reduced
by preventing people from smoking cigarettes. This
was the criterion by which we made our distinction.
And the same goes for our attitude to causes in history. There, too, we distinguish between rational and
accidental causes. The former, since they are potentially applicable to other countries, other periods, and
other conditions, lead to fruitful generalizations and
lessons can be learned from them; they serve the end
of broadening and deepening our understanding.[9] Ac-

---

[9] Professor Popper at one moment stumbles on this point but
fails to see it. Having assumed "a plurality of interpretations which
are fundamentally on the same level of both suggestiveness and ar-

cidental causes cannot be generalized; and, since they are in the fullest sense of the word unique, they teach no lessons and lead to no conclusions. But here I must make another point. It is precisely this notion of an end in view which provides the key to our treatment of causation in history; and this necessarily involves value judgments. Interpretation in history is, as we saw in the last lecture, always bound up with value judgments, and causality is bound up with interpretation. In the words of Meinecke—the "real" Meinecke, the Meinecke of the 1920's—"the search for causalities in history is impossible without reference to values . . . behind the search for causalities there always lies, directly or indirectly, the search for values." [1] And this recalls what I said earlier about the dual and reciprocal function of history—to promote our understanding of the past in the light of the present and of the present in the light of the past. Anything which, like Antony's infatuation with Cleopatra's nose, fails to contribute to this dual purpose is from the point of view of the historian dead and barren.

---

bitrariness" (whatever exactly these two words imply), he adds in a parenthesis that "some of them may be distinguished by their fertility—a point of some importance" (*The Poverty of Historicism*, p. 151). It is not *a* point of some importance: it is *the* point, which proves that "historicism" (in some meanings of the term) is not so poor after all.

[1] *Kausalitäten und Werte in der Geschichte* (1928), translated in Fritz Stern: *Varieties of History* (London: Thames & Hudson; 1957), pp. 268, 273.

At this juncture, it is time for me to confess to a rather shabby trick which I have played on you, though, since you will have had no difficulty in seeing through it, and since it has enabled me on several occasions to shorten and simplify what I had to say, you will perhaps have been indulgent enough to treat it as a convenient piece of shorthand. I have hitherto consistently used the conventional phrase "past and present." But, we all know, the present has no more than a notional existence as an imaginary dividing line between the past and the future. In speaking of the present, I have already smuggled another time dimension into the argument. It would, I think, be easy to show that, since past and future are part of the same time-span, interest in the past and interest in the future are interconnected. The line of demarcation between pre-historic and historical times is crossed when people cease to live only in the present, and become consciously interested both in their past and their future. History begins with the handing down of tradition; and tradition means the carrying of the habits and lessons of the past into the future. Records of the past begin to be kept for the benefit of future generations. "Historical thinking," writes the Dutch historian Huizinga, "is always teleological." [2] Sir Charles Snow recently wrote of Rutherford that "like all scientists . . . he had, almost without thinking

---

[2] J. Huizinga translated in *Varieties of History*, ed. F. Stern (London: Thames & Hudson; 1957), p. 293.

what it meant, the future in his bones." [3] Good historians, I suspect, whether they think about it or not, have the future in their bones. Besides the question: Why? the historian also asks the question: Whither?

---

[3] *The Baldwin Age*, ed. John Raymond (London: Eyre & Spottiswoode; 1960), p. 246.

CHAPTER V

HISTORY AS PROGRESS

LET me begin by quoting a passage from Professor Powicke's inaugural lecture as Regius Professor in Modern History in Oxford thirty years ago:

> The craving for an interpretation of history is so deep-rooted that, unless we have a constructive outlook over the past, we are drawn either to mysticism or to cynicism.[1]

"Mysticism" will, I think, stand for the view that the meaning of history lies somewhere outside history, in the realms of theology or eschatology—the view of such writers as Berdyaev or Niebuhr or Toynbee.[2] "Cynicism" stands for the view, examples of which I have several times quoted, that history has no meaning, or a multiplicity of equally valid or invalid meanings, or the meaning which we arbitrarily choose to give to it. These are perhaps the two most popular views of history today. But I shall unhesitatingly reject both of them. This leaves us with that odd, but suggestive, phrase "a constructive outlook over the past." Having no way of knowing what was in Profes-

---

[1] F. Powicke: *Modern Historians and the Study of History* (London: Odhams Press; 1955), p. 174.

[2] "History passes over into theology," as Toynbee triumphantly asserted (*Civilization on Trial* [London: Oxford University Press; 1948], preface).

sor Powicke's mind when he used the phrase, I shall attempt to read my own interpretation into it.

Like the ancient civilizations of Asia, the classical civilization of Greece and Rome was basically unhistorical. As we have already seen, Herodotus as the father of history had few children; and the writers of classical antiquity were on the whole as little concerned with the future as with the past. Thucydides believed that nothing significant had happened in time before the events which he described, and that nothing significant was likely to happen thereafter. Lucretius deduced man's indifference to the past:

> Consider how that past ages of eternal time before our birth were no concern of ours. This is a mirror which nature holds up to us of future time after our death.[3]

Poetic visions of a brighter future took the form of visions of a return to a golden age of the past—a cyclical view which assimilated the processes of history to the processes of nature. History was not going anywhere: because there was no sense of the past, there was equally no sense of the future. Only Virgil, who in his fourth eclogue had given the classical picture of a return to the golden age, was inspired in the *Aeneid* momentarily to break through the cyclical conception: "*Imperium sine fine dedi*" was a most unclassical thought, which later earned Virgil recognition as a quasi-Christian prophet.

It was the Jews, and after them the Christians, who

---

[3] *De Rerum Natura*, iii, 992–5.

introduced an entirely new element by postulating a goal towards which the historical process is moving— the teleological view of history. History thus acquired a meaning and purpose, but at the expense of losing its secular character. The attainment of the goal of history would automatically mean the end of history: history itself became a theodicy. This was the mediaeval view of history. The Renaissance restored the classical view of an anthropocentric world and of the primacy of reason, but for the pessimistic classical view of the future substituted an optimistic view derived from the Jewish-Christian tradition. Time, which had once been hostile and corroding, now became friendly and creative: contrast Horace's *"Damnosa quid non imminuit dies?"* with Bacon's *"Veritas temporis filia."* The rationalists of the Enlightenment, who were the founders of modern historiography, retained the Jewish-Christian teleological view, but secularized the goal; they were thus enabled to restore the rational character of the historical process itself. History became progress towards the goal of the perfection of man's estate on earth. Gibbon, the greatest of the Enlightenment historians, was not deterred by the nature of his subject from recording what he called "the pleasing conclusion that every age of the world has increased, and still increases, the real wealth, the happiness, the knowledge, and perhaps the virtue, of the human race." [4] The cult of progress reached its

---

[4] Gibbon: *The Decline and Fall of the Roman Empire*, Ch. xxxviii; the occasion of this digression was the downfall of the West-

climax at the moment when British prosperity, power, and self-confidence were at their height; and British writers and British historians were among the most ardent votaries of the cult. The phenomenon is too familiar to need illustration, but I need only quote one or two passages to show how recently faith in progress remained a postulate of all our thinking. Acton, in the report of 1896 on the project of *The Cambridge Modern History* which I quoted in my first lecture, referred to history as "a progressive science"; and in the introduction to the first volume of the history wrote that "we are bound to assume, as the scientific hypothesis on which history is to be written, a progress in human affairs." In the last volume of the history, published in 1910, Dampier, who was a tutor of my college when I was an undergraduate, felt no doubt that "future ages will see no limit to the growth of man's power over the resources of nature and of his intelligent use of them for the welfare of his race." [5] In view of what I am about to say, it is fair for me to admit that this was the atmosphere in which I was educated, and that I could subscribe without reserva-

---

ern empire. A critic in *The Times Literary Supplement*, November 18, 1960, quoting this passage, asks whether Gibbon quite meant it. Of course he did; the point of view of a writer is more likely to reflect the period in which he lives than that about which he writes—a truth well illustrated by this critic, who seeks to transfer his own mid-twentieth century scepticism to a late eighteenth-century writer.

[5] *The Cambridge Modern History: Its Origin, Authorship and Production*, p. 13; *The Cambridge Modern History*, I, p. 4; XII (1910), p. 791.

tion to the words of my senior by half a generation, Bertrand Russell: "I grew up in the full flood of Victorian optimism, and . . . something remains with me of the hopefulness that then was easy." [6]

In 1920, when Bury wrote his book *The Idea of Progress*, a bleaker climate already prevailed, the blame for which he laid, in obedience to the current fashion, on "the doctrinaires who have established the present reign of terror in Russia," though he still described progress as "the animating and controlling idea of Western civilization." [7] Thereafter this note was silent. Nicholas I of Russia is said to have issued an order banning the word "progress": nowadays the philosophers and historians of Western Europe, and even the United States, have come belatedly to agree with him. The hypothesis of progress has been refuted. The decline of the West has become so familiar a phrase that quotation marks are no longer required. But what, apart from all the shouting, has really happened? By whom has this new current of opinion been formed? The other day I was shocked to come across, I think, the only remark of Bertrand Russell I have ever seen which seemed to me to betray an acute sense of class: "There is, on the whole, much less liberty in the world now than there was a hundred years ago." [8] I have no measuring-rod for liberty, and do not know how to balance the lesser liberty of few against

---

[6] Russell: *Portraits From Memory*, p. 17.

[7] Bury: *The Idea of Progress*, pp. vii–viii.

[8] Russell: *Portraits From Memory*, p. 124.

the greater liberty of many. But on any standard of measurement I can only regard the statement as fantastically untrue. I am more attracted by one of those fascinating glimpses which Mr. A. J. P. Taylor sometimes gives us into Oxford academic life. All this talk about the decline of civilization, he writes, "means only that university professors used to have domestic servants and now do their own washing-up." [9] Of course, for former domestic servants, washing-up by professors may be a symbol of progress. The loss of white supremacy in Africa, which worries Empire loyalists, Africaner republicans and investors in gold and copper shares, may look like progress to others. I see no reason why, on this question of progress, I should *ipso facto* prefer the verdict of the 1950's to that of the 1890's, the verdict of the English-speaking world to that of Russia, Asia, and Africa, or the verdict of the middle-class intellectual to that of the man in the street who, according to Mr. Macmillan, has never had it so good. Let us for the moment suspend judgment on the question whether we are living in a period of progress or of decline, and examine a little more closely what is implied in the concept of progress, what assumptions lie behind it, and how far these have become untenable.

I should like, first of all, to clear up the muddle about progress and evolution. The thinkers of the En-

---

[9] *The Observer* (June 21, 1959).

lightenment adopted two apparently incompatible views. They sought to vindicate man's place in the world of nature: the laws of history were equated with the laws of nature. On the other hand, they believed in progress. But what ground was there for treating nature as progressive, as constantly advancing towards a goal? Hegel met the difficulty by sharply distinguishing history, which was progressive, from nature, which was not. The Darwinian revolution appeared to remove all embarrassments by equating evolution and progress: nature, like history, turned out after all to be progressive. But this opened the way to a much graver misunderstanding by confusing biological inheritance, which is the source of evolution, with social acquisition, which is the source of progress in history. The distinction is familiar and obvious. Put a European infant in a Chinese family, and the child will grow up with a white skin, but speaking Chinese. Pigmentation is a biological inheritance, language a social acquisition transmitted by the agency of the human brain. Evolution by inheritance has to be measured in millennia or in millions of years; no measurable biological change is known to have occurred in man since the beginning of written history. Progress by acquisition can be measured in generations. The essence of man as a rational being is that he develops his potential capacities by accumulating the experience of past generations. Modern man is said to have no larger a brain, and no greater innate capacity of thought, than his ancestor 5,000 years ago. But the effectiveness of his thinking has been multiplied many times by learning and incorporating in his experience the experience of the intervening generations. The transmission of acquired characteristics, which is rejected by biologists, is the very foundation of social progress. History is progress through the transmission of acquired skills from one generation to another.

Secondly, we need not and should not conceive progress as having a finite beginning or end. The belief, popular less than fifty years ago, that civilization was invented in the Nile valley in the fourth millennium B.C. is no more credible today than the chronology which placed the creation of the world in 4004 B.C. Civilization, the birth of which we may perhaps take as a starting-point for our hypothesis of progress, was surely not an invention but an infinitely slow process of development, in which spectacular leaps probably occurred from time to time. We need not trouble ourselves with the question when progress—or civilization—began. The hypothesis of a finite end of progress has led to more serious misapprehension. Hegel has been rightly condemned for seeing the end of progress in the Prussian monarchy—apparently the result of an overstrained interpretation of his view of the impossibility of prediction. But Hegel's aberration was capped by that eminent Victorian, Arnold of Rugby, who in his inaugural lecture as Regius Professor of Modern History in Oxford in 1841 thought that modern history would be the last stage in the history of mankind: "It appears to bear marks of the fullness of time, as if there would be no future history beyond it." [1] Marx's prediction that the proletarian revolution would realize the ultimate aim of a classless society was logically and morally less vulnerable; but the presumption of an end of history has an eschatological ring more appropriate to the theologian than to the historian, and reverts to the fallacy of a goal outside history. No doubt a finite end has attractions for the human mind; and Acton's vision of the march of history as an unending progress towards liberty seems chilly and vague. But if the historian is to save his hypothesis of progress, I think he must be prepared to treat it as a process into which the demands and conditions of successive periods will put their own specific content. And this is what is meant by Acton's thesis that history is not only a record of progress, but a "progressive science," or, if you like, that history in both senses of the word—as the course of events and as the record of those events—is progressive. Let us recall Acton's description of the advance of liberty in history:

> It is by the combined efforts of the weak, made under compulsion, to resist the reign of force and constant wrong, that, in the rapid change but slow progress of four hundred years, liberty has been preserved, and secured, and extended, and finally understood.[2]

History as the course of events was conceived by Acton

---

[1] T. Arnold: *An Inaugural Lecture on the Study of Modern History* (1841), p. 38.

[2] Acton: *Lectures on Modern History*, p. 51.

as progress towards liberty, history as the record of those events was progress towards the understanding of liberty: the two processes advanced side by side.[3] The philosopher Bradley, writing in an age when analogies from evolution were fashionable, remarked that "for religious faith the end of evolution is presented as that which . . . is already evolved."[4] For the historian the end of progress is not already evolved. It is something still infinitely remote; and pointers towards it come in sight only as we advance. This does not diminish its importance. A compass is a valuable and indeed indispensable guide. But it is not a chart of the route. The content of history can be realized only as we experience it.

My third point is that no sane person ever believed in a kind of progress which advanced in an unbroken straight line without reverses and deviations and breaks in continuity so that even the sharpest reverse is not necessarily fatal to the belief. Clearly there are periods of regression as well as periods of progress. Moreover, it would be rash to assume that, after a retreat, the advance will be resumed from the same point or along the same line. Hegel's or Marx's four or three civilizations, Toynbee's twenty-one civilizations, the theory of a life-cycle of civilizations passing through rise, decline, and fall—such schemes make no sense in themselves. But they are symptomatic of

---

[3] Mannheim: *Ideology and Utopia*, p. 236, also associates man's "will to shape history" with his "ability to understand it."

[4] F. H. Bradley: *Ethical Studies* (1876), p. 293.

the observed fact that the effort which is needed to drive civilization forward dies away in one place and is later resumed at another, so that whatever progress we can observe in history is certainly not continuous either in time or in place. Indeed, if I were addicted to formulating laws of history, one such law would be to the effect that the group—call it a class, a nation, a continent, a civilization, what you will—which plays the leading role in the advance of civilization in one period is unlikely to play a similar role in the next period, and this for the good reason that it will be too deeply imbued with the traditions, interests, and ideologies of the earlier period to be able to adapt itself to the demands and conditions of the next period.[5] Thus it may very well happen that what seems for one group a period of decline may seem to another the birth of a new advance. Progress does not and cannot mean equal and simultaneous progress for all. It is significant that almost all our latter-day prophets of decline, our sceptics who see no meaning in history and assume that progress is dead, belong to that sector of the world and to that class of society which have triumphantly played a leading and predominant part

---

[5] For a diagnosis of such a situation, see R. S. Lynd: *Knowledge for What?* (Princeton University Press; 1939), p. 88: "Elderly people in our culture are frequently oriented towards the past, the time of their vigour and power, and resist the future as a threat. It is probable that a whole culture in an advanced stage of loss of relative power and disintegration may thus have a dominant orientation towards a lost golden age, while life is lived sluggishly along in the present."

in the advance of civilization for several generations. It is no consolation to them to be told that the role which their group has played in the past will now pass to others. Clearly a history which has played so scurvy a trick on them cannot be a meaningful or rational process. But, if we are to retain the hypothesis of progress, we must, I think, accept the condition of the broken line.

Lastly, I come to the question of what is the essential content of progress in terms of historical action. The people who struggle, say, to extend civil rights to all, or to reform penal practice, or to remove inequalities of race or wealth are consciously seeking to do just those things: they are not consciously seeking to "progress," to realize some historical "law" or "hypothesis" of progress. It is the historian who applies to their actions his hypothesis of progress, and interprets their actions as progress. But this does not invalidate the concept of progress. I am glad on this point to find myself in agreement with Sir Isaiah Berlin that "progress and reaction, however much the words may have been abused, are not empty concepts." [6] It is presupposition of history that man is capable of profiting (not that he necessarily profits) by the experience of his predecessors, and that progress in history, unlike evolution in nature, rests on the transmission of acquired assets. These assets include both material possessions and the capacity to master,

---

[6] *Foreign Affairs*, xxviii, No. 3 (June 1950), p. 382.

transform, and utilize one's environment. Indeed, the two factors are closely interconnected, and react on one another. Marx treats human labour as the foundation of the whole edifice; and this formula seems acceptable if a sufficiently broad sense is attached to "labour." But the mere accumulation of resources will not avail unless it brings with it not only increased technical and social knowledge and experience, but increased mastery of man's environment in the broader sense. At the present time, few people would, I think, question the fact of progress in the accumulation both of material resources and of scientific knowledge, of mastery over the environment in the technological sense. What is questioned is whether there has been in the twentieth century any progress in our ordering of society, in our mastery of the social environment, national or international, whether indeed there has not been a marked regression. Has not the evolution of man as a social being lagged fatally behind the progress of technology?

The symptoms which inspire this question are obvious. But I suspect none the less that it is wrongly put. History has known many turning-points, where the leadership and initiative have passed from one group, from one sector of the world, to another: the period of the rise of the modern state and the shift in the centre of power from the Mediterranean to Western Europe, and the period of the French revolution have been conspicuous modern examples. Such periods are always times of violent upheavals and strug-

gles for power. The old authorities weaken, the old
landmarks disappear; out of a bitter clash of ambitions
and resentments the new order emerges. What I
would suggest is that we are now passing through such
a period. It appears to me simply untrue to say that
our understanding of the problems of social organization or our good will to organize society in the light
of that understanding have regressed: indeed, I should
venture to say that they have greatly increased. It is
not that our capacities have diminished, or our moral
qualities declined. But the period of conflict and upheaval, due to the shifting balance of power between
continents, nations, and classes, through which we are
living has enormously increased the strain on these
capacities and qualities, and limited and frustrated
their effectiveness for positive achievement. While I
do not wish to underestimate the force of the challenge of the past fifty years to the belief in progress
in the Western world, I am still not convinced that
progress in history has come to an end. But, if you
press me further on the content of progress, I think
I can only reply something like this. The notion of a
finite and clearly definable goal of progress in history,
so often postulated by nineteenth-century thinkers,
has proved inapplicable and barren. Belief in progress
means belief not in any automatic or inevitable process, but in the progressive development of human potentialities. Progress is an abstract term; and the concrete ends pursued by mankind arise from time to time
out of the course of history, not from some source

outside it. I profess no belief in the perfectibility of man, or in a future paradise on earth. To this extent I would agree with the theologians and the mystics who assert that perfection is not realizable in history. But I shall be content with the possibility of unlimited progress—or progress subject to no limits that we can need or envisage—towards goals which can be defined only as we advance towards them, and the validity of which can be verified only in a process of attaining them. Nor do I know how, without some such conception of progress, society can survive. Every civilized society imposes sacrifices on the living generation for the sake of generations yet unborn. To justify these sacrifices in the name of a better world in the future is the secular counterpart of justifying them in the name of some divine purpose. In Bury's words, "the principle of duty to posterity is a direct corollary of the idea of progress." [7] Perhaps this duty does not require justification. If it does, I know of no other way to justify it.

This brings me to the famous crux of objectivity in history. The word itself is misleading and question-begging. In an earlier lecture I have already argued that the social sciences—and history among them—cannot accommodate themselves to a theory of knowledge which puts subject and object asunder, and enforces a rigid separation between the observer and the thing observed. We need a new model which does

---

[7] Bury: *The Idea of Progress*, p. ix.

justice to the complex process of interrelation and interaction between them. The facts of history cannot be purely objective, since they become facts of history only in virtue of the significance attached to them by the historian. Objectivity in history—if we are still to use the conventional term—cannot be an objectivity of fact, but only of relation, of the relation between fact and interpretation, between past, present, and future. I need not revert to the reasons which led me to reject as unhistorical the attempt to judge historical events by erecting an absolute standard of value outside history and independent of it. But the concept of absolute truth is also not appropriate to the world of history—or, I suspect, to the world of science. It is only the simplest kind of historical statement that can be adjudged absolutely true or absolutely false. At a more sophisticated level, the historian who contests, say, the verdict of one of his predecessors will normally condemn it, not as absolutely false, but as inadequate or one-sided or misleading, or the product of a point of view which has been rendered obsolete or irrelevant by later evidence. To say that the Russian revolution was due to the stupidity of Nicholas II or to the genius of Lenin is altogether inadequate—so inadequate as to be altogether misleading. But it cannot be called absolutely false. The historian does not deal in absolutes of this kind.

Let us go back to the sad case of Robinson's death. The objectivity of our enquiry into that event depended not on getting our facts right—these were not in dispute—but on distinguishing between the real or significant facts, in which we were interested, and the accidental facts, which we could afford to ignore. We found it easy to draw this distinction because our standard or test of significance, the basis of our objectivity, was clear, and consisted of relevance to the goal in view, *i.e.* reduction of deaths on the roads. But the historian is a less fortunate person than the investigator who has before him the simple and finite purpose of reducing traffic casualties. The historian, too, in his task of interpretation, needs his standard of significance, which is also his standard of objectivity, in order to distinguish between the significant and the accidental; and he, too, can find it only in relevance to the end in view. But this is necessarily an evolving end, since the evolving interpretation of the past is a necessary function of history. The traditional assumption that change has always to be explained in terms of something fixed and unchangeable is contrary to the experience of the historian. "For the historian," says Professor Butterfield, perhaps implicitly reserving for himself a sphere into which historians need not follow him, "the only absolute is change." [8] The abso-

---

[8] Butterfield: *The Whig Interpretation of History*, p. 58. Compare the more elaborate statement in Alfred von Martin: *The Sociology of the Renaissance* [London: Routledge & Kegan Paul; 1945], p. i: "Inertia and motion, static and dynamic, are fundamental categories with which to begin a sociological approach to history. . . . History knows inertia in a relative sense only: the decisive question is whether inertia or change predominates." Change is the positive and absolute, inertia the subjective and relative, element in history.

lute in history is not something in the past from which
we start; it is not something in the present, since all
present thinking is necessarily relative. It is something
still incomplete and in process of becoming—something in the future towards which we move, which
begins to take shape only as we move towards it, and
in the light of which, as we move forward, we gradually shape our interpretation of the past. This is the
secular truth behind the religious myth that the meaning of history will be revealed in the day of judgment.
Our criterion is not an absolute in the static sense of
something that is the same yesterday, today, and for
ever: such an absolute is incompatible with the nature
of history. But it is an absolute in respect of our interpretation of the past. It rejects the relativist view
that one interpretation is as good as another, or that
every interpretation is true in its own time and place,
and it provides the touchstone by which our interpretation of the past will ultimately be judged. It is this
sense of direction in history which alone enables us
to order and interpret the events of the past—the task
of the historian—and to liberate and organize human
energies in the present with a view to the future—the
task of the statesman, the economist, and the social
reformer. But the process itself remains progressive
and dynamic. Our sense of direction, and our interpretation of the past, are subject to constant modification
and evolution as we proceed.

Hegel clothed his absolute in the mystical shape of
a world spirit, and made the cardinal error of bringing

the course of history to an end in the present instead
of projecting it into the future. He recognized a process of continuous evolution in the past, and incon-
gruously denied it in the future. Those who, since
Hegel, have reflected most deeply on the nature of
history have seen in it a synthesis of past and future.
Tocqueville, who did not entirely free himself from
the theological idiom of his day and gave too narrow
content to his absolute, nevertheless had the essence
of the matter. Having spoken of the development of
equality as a universal and permanent phenomenon,
he went on:

> If the men of our time were brought to see the gradual
> and progressive development of equality as at once the
> past and the future of their history, this single discovery
> would give that development the sacred character of the
> will of their lord and master.[9]

An important chapter of history could be written on
that still unfinished theme. Marx, who shared some
of Hegel's inhibitions about looking into the future,
and was principally concerned to root his teaching
firmly in past history, was compelled by the nature of
his theme to project into the future his absolute of the
classless society. Bury described the idea of progress,
a little awkwardly, but clearly with the same intention,
as "a theory which involves a synthesis of the past and
a prophecy of the future." [1] Historians, says Namier in

---

[9] Alexis de Tocqueville: Preface to *Democracy in America*.
[1] Bury: *The Idea of Progress*, p. 5.

a deliberately paradoxical phrase, which he proceeds to illustrate with his usual wealth of examples, "imagine the past and remember the future." [2] Only the future can provide the key to the interpretation of the past; and it is only in this sense that we can speak of an ultimate objectivity in history. It is at once the justification and the explanation of history that the past throws light on the future, and the future throws light on the past.

What, then, do we mean when we praise a historian for being objective, or say that one historian is more objective than another? Not, it is clear, simply that he gets his facts right, but rather that he chooses the right facts, or, in other words, that he applies the right standard of significance. When we call a historian objective, we mean, I think, two things. First of all, we mean that he has a capacity to rise above the limited vision of his own situation in society and in history— a capacity which, as I suggested in an earlier lecture, is partly dependent on his capacity to recognize the extent of his involvement in that situation, to recognize, that is to say, the impossibility of total objectivity. Secondly, we mean that he has the capacity to project his vision into the future in such a way as to give him a more profound and more lasting insight into the past than can be attained by those historians whose outlook is entirely bounded by their own immediate situation. No historian today will echo Ac-

[2] Namier: *Conflicts* (London: Macmillan & Co.; 1942), p. 70.

ton's confidence in the prospect of "ultimate history." But some historians write history which is more durable, and has more of this ultimate and objective character, than others; and these are the historians who have what I may call a long-term vision over the past and over the future. The historian of the past can make an approach towards objectivity only as he approaches towards the understanding of the future.

When, therefore, I spoke of history in an earlier lecture as a dialogue between past and present, I should rather have called it a dialogue between the events of the past and progressively emerging future ends. The historian's interpretation of the past, his selection of the significant and the relevant, evolves with the progressive emergence of new goals. To take the simplest of all illustrations, so long as the main goal appeared to be the organization of constitutional liberties and political rights, the historian interpreted the past in constitutional and political terms. When economic and social ends began to replace constitutional and political ends, historians turned to economic and social interpretations of the past. In this process, the sceptic might plausibly allege that the new interpretation is no truer than the old; each is true for its period. Nevertheless, since the preoccupation with economic and social ends represents a broader and more advanced stage in human development than the preoccupation with political and constitutional ends, so the economic and social interpretation of history may be said to represent a more advanced stage in history than the exclusively political interpretation. The old interpretation is not rejected, but is both included and superseded in the new. Historiography is a progressive science in the sense that it seeks to provide constantly expanding and deepening insights into a course of events which is itself progressive. This is what I should mean by saying that we need "a constructive outlook over the past." Modern historiography has grown up during the past two centuries in this dual belief in progress, and cannot survive without it, since it is this belief which provides it with its standard of significance, its touchstone for distinguishing between the real and the accidental. Goethe, in a conversation towards the end of his life, cut the Gordian knot a little brusquely:

When eras are on the decline, all tendencies are subjective; but on the other hand when matters are ripening for a new epoch, all tendencies are objective.[8]

Nobody is obliged to believe either in the future of history or in the future of society. It is possible that our society may be destroyed or may perish of slow decay, and that history may relapse into theology—that is to say, a study not of human achievement, but of the divine purpose—or into literature—that is to say, a telling of stories and legends without purpose

---

[8] Quoted in J. Huizinga: *Men and Ideas* (New York: Meridian Books; 1959), p. 50.

or significance. But this will not be history in the sense in which we have known it in the last two hundred years.

I have still to deal with the familiar and popular objection to any theory which finds the ultimate criterion of historical judgment in the future. Such a theory, it is said, implies that success is the ultimate criterion of judgment, and that, if not whatever is, whatever will be, is right. For the past two hundred years most historians have not only assumed a direction in which history is moving, but have consciously or unconsciously believed that this direction was on the whole the right direction, that mankind was moving from the worse to the better, from the lower to the higher. The historian not only recognized the direction, but endorsed it. The test of significance which he applied in his approach to the past was not only a sense of the course on which history was moving, but a sense of his own moral involvement in that course. The alleged dichotomy between the "is" and the "ought," between fact and value, was resolved. It was an optimistic view, a product of an age of overwhelming confidence in the future; Whigs and Liberals, Hegelians and Marxists, theologians and rationalists, remained firmly, and more or less articulately, committed to it. For two hundred years it could have been described without much exaggeration as the accepted and implicit answer to the question: What is history? The reaction against it has come with the current mood of apprehension and pessimism, which has left the field clear for the theologians who seek the meaning of history outside history, and for the sceptics who find no meaning in history at all. We are assured on all hands, and with the utmost emphasis, that the dichotomy between "is" and "ought" is absolute and cannot be resolved, that "values" cannot be derived from "facts." This is, I think, a false trail. Let us see how a few historians, or writers about history, chosen more or less at random, have felt about this question.

Gibbon justifies the amount of space devoted in his narrative to the victories of Islam on the ground that "the disciples of Mohammed still hold the civil and religious sceptre of the Oriental world." But, he adds, "the same labour would be unworthily bestowed on the swarms of savages who, between the 7th and 12th centuries, descended from the plains of Scythia," since "the majesty of the Byzantine throne repelled and survived these disorderly attacks." [4] This seems not unreasonable. History is, by and large, a record of what people did, not of what they failed to do: to this extent it is inevitably a success story. Professor Tawney remarks that historians give "an appearance of inevitableness" to an existing order "by dragging into

[4] Gibbon: *The Decline and Fall of the Roman Empire,* Ch. lv.

prominence the forces which have triumphed and thrusting into the background those which they have swallowed up." [5] But is not this in a sense the essence of the historian's job? The historian must not under-estimate the opposition; he must not represent the victory as a walk-over if it was touch-and-go. Some-times those who were defeated have made as great a contribution to the ultimate result as the victors. These are familiar maxims to every historian. But, by and large, the historian is concerned with those who, whether victorious or defeated, achieved some-thing. I am not a specialist in the history of cricket. But its pages are presumably studded with the names of those who made centuries rather than of those who made ducks and were left out of the side. Hegel's famous statement that in history "only those peoples can come under our notice which form a state," [6] has been justly criticized as attach-ing an exclusive value to one form of social organiza-tion and paving the way for an obnoxious state-worship. But, in principle, what Hegel is trying to say is correct, and reflects the familiar distinction between pre-history and history; only those peoples which have succeeded in organizing their society in some degree cease to be primitive savages and enter into history. Carlyle, in his *French Revolution*, called Louis XV

---

[5] R. H. Tawney: *The Agrarian Problem in the Sixteenth Century* (London: Longmans, Green & Co.; 1912), p. 177.

[6] *Lectures on the Philosophy of History* (Eng. transl., 1884), p. 40.

"a very World Solecism incarnate." He evidently liked the phrase, for he embroidered it later in a longer passage:

What new universal vertiginous movement is this: of institutions, social arrangements, individual minds, which once worked co-operative, now rolling and grinding in distracted collision? Inevitable; it is the breaking-up of a World Solecism, worn out at last.[7]

The criterion is once more historical: what fitted one epoch had become a solecism in another, and is condemned on that account. Even Sir Isaiah Berlin, when he descends from the heights of philosophical abstraction and considers concrete historical situations, appears to have come round to this view. In a broadcast delivered some time after the publication of his essay on *Historical Inevitability*, he praised Bismarck, in spite of moral shortcomings, as a "genius" and "the greatest example in the last century of a politician of the highest powers of political judgment," and contrasted him favourably in this respect with such men as Joseph II of Austria, Robespierre, Lenin, and Hitler, who failed to realize "their positive ends." I find this verdict odd. But what interests me at the moment is the criterion of judgment. Bismarck, says Sir Isaiah, understood the material in which he was working; the others were led away by abstract theories which failed to work. The moral is that "failure comes from resisting that which works best . . . in favour of some sys-

---

[7] T. Carlyle: *The French Revolution*, I, i, Ch. 4; I, iii, Ch. 7.

tematic method or principle claiming universal validity." [8] In other words, the criterion of judgment in history is not some "principle claiming universal validity," but "that which works best."

It is not only—I need hardly say—when analysing the past that we invoke this criterion of "what works best." If someone informed you that he thought that, at the present juncture, the union of Great Britain and the United States of America in a single state under a single sovereignty was desirable, you might agree that this was quite a sensible view. If he went on to say that constitutional monarchy was preferable to presidential democracy as a form of government, you might also agree that this was quite sensible. But suppose he then told you that he proposed to devote himself to conducting a campaign for the reunion of the two countries under the British crown; you would probably reply that he would be wasting his time. If you tried to explain why, you would have to tell him that issues of this kind have to be debated on the basis not of some principle of general application, but of what would work in given historical conditions; you might even commit the cardinal sin of speaking of history with a capital H and tell him that History was against him. The business of the politician is to consider not merely what is morally or theoretically desirable, but also the forces which exist in the world, and how they can be directed or manipulated to prob-

---

[8] Broadcast on "Political Judgment" in the Third Programme of the B.B.C., June 19, 1957.

ably partial realizations of the ends in view. Our political decisions taken in the light of our interpretation
of history are rooted in this compromise. But our interpretation of history is rooted in the same compromise. Nothing is more radically false than to set up
some supposedly abstract standard of the desirable and
condemn the past in the light of it. For the word "success," which has come to have invidious connotations,
let us by all means substitute the neutral "that which
works best." Since I have joined issue with Sir Isaiah
Berlin on several occasions during these lectures, I am
glad to be able to close the account with, at any rate,
this measure of agreement.

But acceptance of the criterion of "what works
best" does not make its application either easy or self-
evident. It is not a criterion which encourages snap
verdicts, or which bows down to the view that what is,
is right. Pregnant failures are not unknown in history.
History recognizes what I may call "delayed achievement": the apparent failures of today may turn out
to have made a vital contribution to the achievement
of tomorrow—prophets born before their time. Indeed, one of the advantages of this criterion over the
criterion of a supposedly fixed and universal principle
is that it may require us to postpone our judgment or
to qualify it in the light of things that have not yet
happened. Proudhon, who talked freely in terms of
abstract moral principles, condoned the *coup d'état*
of Napoleon III after it had succeeded; Marx, who
rejected the criterion of abstract moral principles, con-

demned Proudhon for condoning it. Looking back
from a longer historical perspective, we shall probably
agree that Proudhon was wrong and Marx right. The
achievement of Bismarck provides an excellent starting-point for an examination of this problem of historical judgment; and, while I accept Sir Isaiah's criterion of "what works best," I am still puzzled by the
narrow and short-term limits within which he is
apparently content to apply it. Did what Bismarck
created really work well? I should have thought that
it led to an immense disaster. This does not mean that
I am seeking to condemn Bismarck who created the
German Reich, or the mass of Germans who wanted
it and helped to create it. But, as a historian, I still
have many questions to ask. Did the eventual disaster
occur because some hidden flaws existed in the structure of the Reich? or because something in the in-
ternal conditions which brought it to birth destined it
to become self-assertive and aggressive? or because,
when the Reich was created, the European or world
scene was already so crowded, and expansive tendencies among the existing Great Powers already so
strong, that the emergence of another expansive Great
Power was sufficient to cause a major collision and
bring down the whole system in ruins? On the last
hypothesis, it may be wrong to hold Bismarck and
the German people responsible, or solely responsible,
for the disaster: you cannot really blame the last
straw. But an objective judgment on Bismarck's
achievement and how it worked awaits an answer from

the historian to these questions, and I am not sure that he is yet in a position to answer them all definitively. What I would say is that the historian of the 1920's was nearer to objective judgment than the historian of the 1880's, and that the historian of today is nearer than the historian of the 1920's; the historian of the year 2000 may be nearer still. This illustrates my thesis that objectivity in history does not and cannot rest on some fixed and immovable standard of judgment existing here and now, but only on a standard which is laid up in the future and is evolved as the course of history advances. History acquires meaning and objectivity only when it establishes a coherent relation between past and future.

Let us now take another look at this alleged dichotomy between fact and value. Values cannot be derived from facts. This statement is partly true, but partly false. You have only to examine the system of values prevailing in any period or in any country to realize how much of it is moulded by the facts of the environment. In an earlier lecture I drew attention to the changing historical content of value-words like liberty, equality, or justice. Or take the Christian church as an institution largely concerned with the propagation of moral values. Contrast the values of primitive Christianity with those of the mediaeval papacy, or the values of the mediaeval papacy with those of the Protestant churches of the nineteenth century. Or contrast the values promulgated today by, say, the Christian church in Spain with the values

promulgated by the Christian churches in the United
States. These differences in values spring from differences of historical fact. Or consider the historical facts
which in the last century and a half have caused slavery or racial inequality or the exploitation of child
labour—all once accepted as morally neutral or reputable—to be generally regarded as immoral. The
proposition that values cannot be derived from facts
is, to say the least, one-sided and misleading. Or let us
reverse the statement. Facts cannot be derived from
values. This is partly true, but may also be misleading,
and requires qualification. When we seek to know
the facts, the questions which we ask, and therefore
the answers which we obtain, are prompted by our
system of values. Our picture of the facts of our environment is moulded by our values, *i.e.* by the categories through which we approach the facts; and this
picture is one of the important facts which we have to
take into account. Values enter into the facts and are
an essential part of them. Our values are an essential
part of our equipment as human beings. It is through
our values that we have that capacity to adapt ourselves to our environment, and to adapt our environment to ourselves, to acquire that mastery over our
environment, which has made history a record of progress. But do not, in dramatizing the struggle of man
with his environment, set up a false antithesis and a
false separation between facts and values. Progress in
history is achieved through the interdependence and
interaction of facts and values. The objective historian

is the historian who penetrates most deeply into this reciprocal process.

A clue to this problem of facts and values is provided by our ordinary use of the word "truth"—a word which straddles the world of fact and the world of value and is made up of elements of both. Nor is this an idiosyncrasy of the English language. The words for truth in the Latin languages, the German *Wahrheit*, the Russian *pravda*,[9] all possess this dual character. Every language appears to require this word for a truth which is not merely a statement of fact and not merely a value judgment, but embraces both elements. It may be a fact that I went to London last week. But you would not ordinarily call it a truth: it is devoid of any value content. On the other hand, when the Founding Fathers of the United States in the Declaration of Independence referred to the self-evident truth that all men are created equal, you may feel that the value content of the statement predominates over the factual content, and may on that account challenge its right to be regarded as a truth. Somewhere between these two poles—the north pole of valueless facts and the south pole of value judgments still struggling to transform themselves into facts—lies the realm of historical truth. The historian, as I said in my first lecture, is balanced between fact and interpretation, be-

---

[9] The case of *pravda* is especially interesting since there is another old Russian word for truth, *istina*. But the distinction is not between truth as fact and truth as value; *pravda* is human truth in both aspects, *istina* divine truth in both aspects—truth about God and truth as revealed by God.

tween fact and value. He cannot separate them. It may be that, in a static world, you are obliged to pronounce a divorce between fact and value. But history is meaningless in a static world. History in its essence is change, movement or—if you do not cavil at the old-fashioned word—progress.

I return therefore in conclusion to Acton's description of progress as "the scientific hypothesis on which history is to be written." You can, if you please, turn history into theology by making the meaning of the past depend on some extra-historical and super-rational power. You can, if you please, turn it into literature—a collection of stories and legends about the past without meaning or significance. History properly so-called can be written only by those who find and accept a sense of direction in history itself. The belief that we have come from somewhere is closely linked with the belief that we are going somewhere. A society which has lost belief in its capacity to progress in the future will quickly cease to concern itself with its progress in the past. As I said at the beginning of my first lecture, our view of history reflects our view of society. I now come back to my starting-point by declaring my faith in the future of society and in the future of history.

CHAPTER VI

THE WIDENING HORIZON

THE conception which I have put forward in these lectures of history as a constantly moving process, with the historian moving within it, seems to commit me to some concluding reflexions on the position of history and of the historian in our time. We live in an epoch when—not for the first time in history—predictions of world catastrophe are in the air, and weigh heavily on all. They can be neither proved nor disproved. But they are at any rate far less certain than the prediction that we shall all die; and, since the certainty of that prediction does not prevent us from laying plans for our own future, so I shall proceed to discuss the present and future of our society on the assumption that this country—or, if not this country, some major part of the world—will survive the hazards that threaten us, and that history will continue.

The middle years of the twentieth century find the world in a process of change probably more profound and more sweeping than any which has overtaken it since the mediaeval world broke up in ruins and the foundations of the modern world were laid in the fifteenth and sixteenth centuries. The change is no doubt ultimately the product of scientific discoveries and inventions, of their ever more widespread application, and of developments arising directly or indirectly out of them. The most conspicuous aspect of the change is a social revolution comparable with that which, in the fifteenth and sixteenth centuries, inaugurated the rise to power of a new class based on finance and commerce, and later on industry. The new structure of our industry and the new structure of our society present problems too vast for me to embark on here. But the change has two aspects more immediately relevant to my theme—what I may call a change in depth, and a change in geographical extent. I will attempt to touch briefly on both of these.

History begins when men begin to think of the passage of time in terms not of natural processes—the cycle of the seasons, the human life-span—but of a series of specific events in which men are consciously involved and which they can consciously influence. History, says Burckhardt, is "the break with nature caused by the awakening of consciousness." [1] History is the long struggle of man, by the exercise of his reason, to understand his environment and to act upon it. But the modern period has broadened the struggle in a revolutionary way. Man now seeks to understand, and to act on, not only his environment, but himself; and this has added, so to speak, a new dimension to reason, and a new dimension to history. The present

---

[1] Burckhardt: *Reflections on History* (London: George Allen & Unwin; 1959), p. 31.

age is the most historically minded of all ages. Modern man is to an unprecedented degree self-conscious and therefore conscious of history. He peers eagerly back into the twilight out of which he has come in the hope that its faint beams will illuminate the obscurity into which he is going; and, conversely, his aspirations and anxieties about the path that lies ahead quicken his insight into what lies behind. Past, present, and future are linked together in the endless chain of history.

The change in the modern world which consisted in the development of man's consciousness of himself may be said to begin with Descartes, who first established man's position as a being who can not only think, but think about his own thinking, who can observe himself in the act of observing, so that man is simultaneously the subject and the object of thought and observation. But the development did not become fully explicit till the latter part of the eighteenth century, when Rousseau opened up new depths of human self-understanding and self-consciousness, and gave man a new outlook on the world of nature and on traditional civilization. The French revolution, said Tocqueville, was inspired by "the belief that what was wanted was to replace the complex of traditional customs governing the social order of the day by simple, elementary rules deriving from the exercise of the human reason and from natural law." [2] "Never till then," wrote Acton in one of his manuscript notes, "had men

---

[2] Tocqueville: *De l'Ancien Régime*, III, Ch. 1.

sought liberty, knowing what they sought." [3] For
Acton, as for Hegel, liberty and reason were never far
apart. And with the French revolution was linked the
American revolution.

Fourscore and seven years ago our fathers brought forth
upon this continent a new nation conceived in liberty and
dedicated to the proposition that all men are created
equal.

It was, as Lincoln's words suggest, a unique event—
the first occasion in history when men deliberately
and consciously formed themselves into a nation, and
then consciously and deliberately set out to mould
other men into it. In the seventeenth and eighteenth
centuries man had already become fully conscious of
the world around him and of its laws. They were no
longer the mysterious decrees of an inscrutable providence, but laws accessible to reason. But they were
laws to which man was subject, and not laws of his
own making. In the next stage man was to become
fully conscious of his power over his environment and
over himself and of his right to make the laws under
which he would live.

The transition from the eighteenth century to the
modern world was long and gradual. Its representative
philosophers were Hegel and Marx, both of whom
occupy an ambivalent position. Hegel is rooted in the
idea of laws of providence converted into laws of reason. Hegel's world spirit grasps providence firmly with

---

[3] Cambridge University Library: Add. MSS. 4870.

one hand and reason with the other. He echoes Adam Smith. Individuals "gratify their own interests; but something more is thereby accomplished which is latent in this action though not present in their consciousness." Of the rational purpose of the world spirit he writes that men, "in the very act of realizing it, make it the occasion of satisfying their desire, whose import is different from that purpose." This is simply the harmony of interests translated into the language of German philosophy.[4] Hegel's equivalent for Smith's "hidden hand" was the famous "cunning of reason" which sets men to work to fulfil purposes of which they are not conscious. But Hegel was none the less the philosopher of the French revolution, the first philosopher to see the essence of reality in historical change and in the development of man's consciousness of himself. Development in history meant development towards the concept of freedom. But, after 1815, the inspiration of the French revolution fizzled out in the doldrums of the Restoration. Hegel was politically too timid and, in his later years, too firmly entrenched in the Establishment of his day to introduce any concrete meaning into his metaphysical propositions. Herzen's description of Hegel's doctrines as "the algebra of Revolution" was singularly apt. Hegel provided the notation, but gave it no practical content. It was left for Marx to write the arithmetic into Hegel's algebraical equations.

---

[4] The quotations are from Hegel's *Philosophy of History*.

A disciple both of Adam Smith and of Hegel, Marx
started from the conception of a world ordered by
rational laws of nature. Like Hegel, but this time in a
practical and concrete form, he made the transition to
the conception of a world ordered by laws evolving
through a rational process in response to man's revolutionary initiative. In Marx's final synthesis history
meant three things, which were inseparable one from
another and formed a coherent and rational whole:
the motion of events in accordance with objective, and
primarily economic, laws; the corresponding development of thought through a dialectical process; and
corresponding action in the form of the class struggle
which reconciles and unites the theory and practice of
revolution. What Marx offers is a synthesis of objective
laws and of conscious action to translate them into
practice, of what are sometimes (though misleadingly)
called determinism and voluntarism. Marx constantly
writes of laws to which men have hitherto been subject
without being conscious of them; he more than once
drew attention to what he called the "false consciousness" of those enmeshed in a capitalist economy and
capitalist society: "the conceptions formed about the
laws of production in the minds of the agents of production and circulation will differ widely from the real
laws." [5] But one finds in Marx's writings striking examples of calls for conscious revolutionary action.
"Philosophers have only interpreted the world differ-

---

[5] *Capital*, iii (Engl. transl., 1909), 369.

ently," ran the famous thesis on Feuerbach; "but the point is to change it." "The proletariat," declared the *Communist Manifesto*, "will use its political dominance to strip the bourgeoisie step by step of all capital, and concentrate all means of production in the hands of the state." And in *The Eighteenth Brumaire of Louis Bonaparte*, Marx spoke of "intellectual self-consciousness dissolving by a century-old process all traditional ideas." It was the proletariat which would dissolve the false consciousness of capitalist society and introduce the true consciousness of the classless society. But the failure of the revolutions of 1848 was a serious and dramatic set-back to developments which had seemed imminent when Marx began to work. The latter part of the nineteenth century passed in an atmosphere which was still predominantly one of prosperity and security. It was not till the turn of the century that we complete the transition to the contemporary period of history, in which the primary function of reason is no longer to understand objective laws governing the behaviour of man in society, but rather to re-shape society and the individuals who compose it by conscious action. In Marx, "class," though not precisely defined, remains on the whole an objective conception to be established by economic analysis. In Lenin, the emphasis shifts from "class" to "party," which constitutes the vanguard of the class and infuses into it the necessary element of class-consciousness. In Marx, "ideology" is a negative term—a product of the false consciousness of the capitalist order of society. In

Lenin, "ideology" becomes neutral or positive—a belief implanted by an *élite* of class-conscious leaders
into a mass of potentially class-conscious workers. The
moulding of class-consciousness is no longer an automatic process, but a job to be undertaken.

The other great thinker who has added a fresh dimension to reason in our time is Freud. Freud remains
today a somewhat enigmatic figure. He was by training
and background a nineteenth-century liberal individualist, and accepted without question the common,
but misleading, assumption of a fundamental antithesis between the individual and society. Freud, approaching man as a biological rather than as a social
entity, tended to treat the social environment as something historically given rather than as something in
constant process of creation and transformation by
man himself. He has always been attacked by the
Marxists for approaching what are really social problems from the standpoint of the individual, and condemned as a reactionary on that account; and this
charge, which was valid only in part against Freud
himself, has been much more fully justified by the current neo-Freudian school in the United States, which
assumes that maladjustments are inherent in the individual and not in the structure of society, and treats
the adaptation of the individual to society as the essential function of psychology. The other popular charge
against Freud, that he has extended the role of the irrational in human affairs, is totally false, and rests on a
crude confusion between recognition of the irrational

element in human behaviour and a cult of the irrational. That a cult of the irrational does exist in the
English-speaking world today, mainly in the form of a
depreciation of the achievements and potentialities of
reason, is unfortunately true; it is part of the current
wave of pessimism and ultra-conservatism, of which I
will speak later. But this does not stem from Freud,
who was an unqualified and rather primitive rational-
ist. What Freud did was to extend the range of our
knowledge and understanding by opening up the unconscious roots of human behaviour to consciousness
and to rational enquiry. This was an extension of the
domain of reason, an increase in man's power to
understand and control himself, and therefore his environment; and it represents a revolutionary and progressive achievement. In this respect, Freud comple-
ments, and does not contradict, the work of Marx.
Freud belongs to the contemporary world in the sense
that, though he himself did not entirely escape from
the conception of a fixed and invariable human nature,
he provided tools for a deeper understanding of the
roots of human behaviour and thus for its conscious
modification through rational processes.

For the historian Freud's special significance is twofold. In the first place, Freud has driven the last nail
into the coffin of the ancient illusion that the motives
from which men allege or believe themselves to have
acted are in fact adequate to explain their action: this
is a negative achievement of some importance, though
the positive claim of some enthusiasts to throw light

on the behaviour of the great men of history by the
methods of psychoanalysis should be taken with a
pinch of salt. The procedure of psychoanalysis rests on
the cross-examination of the patient who is being investigated: you cannot cross-examine the dead. Secondly, Freud, reinforcing the work of Marx, has encouraged the historian to examine himself and his own
position in history, the motives—perhaps hidden
motives—which have guided his choice of theme or
period and his selection and interpretation of the facts,
the national and social background which has determined his angle of vision, the conception of the future
which shapes his conception of the past. Since Marx
and Freud wrote, the historian has no excuse to think
of himself as a detached individual standing outside
society and outside history. This is the age of self-
consciousness: the historian can and should know
what he is doing.

This transition to what I have called the contemporary world—the extension to new spheres of the function and power of reason—is not yet complete: it is
part of the revolutionary change through which the
twentieth-century world is passing. I should like to
examine some of the main symptoms of the transition.

Let me begin with economics. Down to 1914 belief
in objective economic laws, which governed the economic behaviour of men and nations, and which they
could defy only to their own detriment, was still virtually unchallenged. Trade cycles, price fluctuations, unemployment were determined by those laws. As late

as 1930, when the great depression set in, this was still the dominant view. Thereafter things moved fast. In the 1930's, people began to talk of "the end of economic man," meaning the man who consistently pursued his economic interests in accordance with economic laws; and since then nobody, except a few Rip Van Winkles of the nineteenth century, believes in economic laws in this sense. Today economics has become either a series of theoretical mathematical equations, or a practical study of how some people push others around. The change is mainly a product of the transition from individual to large-scale capitalism. So long as the individual entrepreneur and merchant predominated, nobody seemed in control of the economy or capable of influencing it in any significant way; and the illusion of impersonal laws and processes was preserved. Even the Bank of England, in the days of its greatest power, was thought of not as a skilful operator and manipulator, but as an objective and quasi-automatic registrar of economic trends. But with the transition from a *laissez-faire* economy to a managed economy (whether a managed capitalist economy or a socialist economy, whether the management is done by large-scale capitalist, and nominally private, concerns or by the state), this illusion is dissolved. It becomes clear that certain people are taking certain decisions for certain ends; and that these decisions set our economic course for us. Everyone knows today that the price of oil or soap does not vary in response to some objective law of supply and demand. Everyone knows,

or thinks he knows, that slumps and unemployment
are man-made: governments admit, indeed claim, that
they know how to cure them. The transition has been
made from *laissez-faire* to planning, from the unconscious to the self-conscious, from belief in objective
economic laws to belief that man by his own action
can be the master of his economic destiny. Social policy
has gone hand in hand with economic policy: indeed
economic policy has been incorporated in social policy.
Let me quote from the last volume of the first *Cambridge Modern History*, published in 1910, a highly
perceptive comment from a writer who was anything
but a Marxist and had probably never heard of Lenin:

> The belief in the possibility of social reform by con-
> scious effort is the dominant current of the European
> mind; it has superseded the belief in liberty as the one
> panacea. . . . Its currency in the present is as significant
> and as pregnant as the belief in the rights of man about
> the time of the French revolution.[6]

Today, fifty years after this passage was written, more
than forty years after the Russian revolution, and
thirty years after the great depression, this belief has
become a commonplace; and the transition from submission to objective economic laws which, though supposedly rational, were beyond man's control, to belief
in the capacity of man to control his economic destiny
by conscious action seems to me to represent an ad-

---

[6] *The Cambridge Modern History*, XII (1910), p. 15. The author
of the chapter was S. Leathes, one of the editors of the *History*,
and a Civil Service Commissioner.

vance in the application of reason to human affairs, an increased capacity in man to understand and master himself and his environment, which I should be prepared, if necessary, to call by the old-fashioned name of progress.

I have no space to touch in detail on the similar processes at work in other fields. Even science, as we have seen, is now less concerned to investigate and establish objective laws of nature, than to frame working hypotheses by which man may be enabled to harness nature to his purposes and transform his environment. More significant, man has begun, through the conscious exercise of reason, not only to transform his environment but to transform himself. At the end of the eighteenth century Malthus, in an epoch-making work, attempted to establish objective laws of population working, like Adam Smith's laws of the market, without anyone's being conscious of the process. To-day nobody believes in such objective laws; but the control of population has become a matter of rational and conscious social policy. We have seen in our time the lengthening by human effort of the span of human life and the altering of the balance between the generations in our population. We have heard of drugs consciously used to influence human behaviour, and surgical operations designed to alter human character. Both man and society have changed, and have been changed by conscious human effort, before our eyes. But the most significant of these changes have probably been those brought about by the development and

use of modern methods of persuasion and indoctrina-
tion. Educators at all levels are nowadays more and
more consciously concerned to make their contribution to the shaping of society in a particular mould,
and to inculcate in the rising generation the attitudes,
loyalties, and opinions appropriate to that type of society; educational policy is an integral part of any rationally planned social policy. The primary function of
reason, as applied to man in society, is no longer
merely to investigate, but to transform; and this
heightened consciousness of the power of man to improve the management of his social, economic, and
political affairs by the application of rational processes
seems to me one of the major aspects of the twentieth-
century revolution.

This expansion of reason is merely part of the process which I called in an earlier lecture "individualization"—the diversification of individual skills and occupations and opportunities which is the concomitant of
an advancing civilization. Perhaps the most far-reaching social consequence of the industrial revolution has
been the progressive increase in the numbers of those
who learn to think, to use their reason. In Great Britain our passion for gradualism is such that the movement is sometimes scarcely perceptible. We have
rested on the laurels of universal elementary education
for the best part of a century, and have still not advanced very far or very quickly towards universal
higher education. This did not matter so much when
we led the world. It matters more when we are being

overtaken by others in a greater hurry than ourselves, and when the pace has everywhere been speeded up by technological change. For the social revolution and the technological revolution and the scientific revolution are part and parcel of the same process. If you want an academic example of the process of individualization, consider the immense diversification over the past fifty or sixty years of history, or of science, or any particular science, and the enormously increased variety of individual specializations which it offers. But I have a far more striking example of the process at a different level. More than thirty years ago a high German military officer visiting the Soviet Union listened to some illuminating remarks from a Soviet officer concerned with the building up of the Red air force:

We Russians have to do with still primitive human material. We are compelled to adapt the flying machine to the type of flyer who is at our disposal. To the extent to which we are successful in developing a new type of men, the technical development of the material will also be perfected. The two factors condition each other. Primitive men cannot be put into complicated machines.[7]

Today, a bare generation later, we know that Russian machines are no longer primitive, and that millions of Russian men and women who plan, build, and operate these machines are no longer primitive, either. As a historian, I am more interested in this latter phenomenon. The rationalization of production means something far more important—the rationalization of man.

[7] *Vierteljahrshefte für Zeitgeschichte* (Munich), I (1953), p. 38.

All over the world today primitive men are learning to use complicated machines, and in doing so are learning to think, to use their reason. The revolution, which you may justly call a social revolution, but which I call in the present context the expansion of reason, is only just beginning. But it is advancing at a staggering pace to keep abreast of the staggering technological advances of the last generation. It seems to me one of the major aspects of our twentieth-century revolution.

Some of our pessimists and sceptics will certainly call me to order if I fail at this point to notice the dangers and the ambiguous aspects of the role assigned to reason in the contemporary world. In an earlier lecture I pointed out that increasing individualization in the sense described did not imply any weakening of social pressures for conformity and uniformity. This is, indeed, one of the paradoxes of our complex modern society. Education, which is a necessary and powerful instrument in promoting the expansion of individual capacities and opportunities, and therefore of increasing individualization, is also a powerful instrument in the hands of interested groups for promoting social uniformity. Pleas frequently heard for more responsible broadcasting and television, or for a more responsible press, are directed in the first instance against certain negative phenomena which it is easy to condemn. But they quickly become pleas to use these powerful instruments of mass persuasion in order to inculcate desirable tastes and desirable opinions— the standard of desirability being found in the accepted tastes and opinions of the society. Such campaigns, in the hands of those who promote them, are conscious and rational processes designed to shape society, by shaping its individual members, in a desired direction. Other glaring examples of these dangers are provided by the commercial advertiser and the political propagandist. The two roles are, indeed, frequently doubled; openly in the United States, and rather more sheepishly in Great Britain, parties and candidates employ professional advertisers to put themselves across. The two procedures, even when formally distinct, are remarkably similar. Professional advertisers and the heads of the propaganda departments of great political parties are highly intelligent men who bring all the resources of reason to bear on their task. Reason, however, as in the other instances we have examined is employed not for mere exploration but constructively, not statically but dynamically. Professional advertisers and campaign managers are not primarily concerned with existing facts. They are interested in what the consumer or elector now believes or wants only in so far as this enters into the end-product, *i.e.* what the consumer or elector can by skilful handling be induced to believe or want. Moreover, their study of mass psychology has shown them that the most rapid way to secure acceptance of their views is through an appeal to the irrational element in the make-up of the customer and elector, so that the picture which confronts us is one in which an *élite* of professional industrialists or party leaders through rational processes more highly

developed than ever before attains its ends by understanding and trading on the irrationalism of the
masses. The appeal is not primarily to reason: it proceeds in the main by the method which Oscar Wilde
called "hitting below the intellect." I have somewhat
overdrawn the picture lest I should be accused of un-
der-estimating the danger.[8] But it is broadly correct,
and could easily be applied to other spheres. In every
society, more or less coercive measures are applied by
ruling groups to organize and control mass opinion.
This method seems worse than some because it constitutes an abuse of reason.

In reply to this serious and well-founded indictment
I have only two arguments. The first is the familiar one
that every invention, every innovation, every new technique discovered in the course of history has had its
negative as well as its positive sides. The cost has always to be borne by somebody. I do not know how
long it was after the invention of printing before critics
began to point out that it facilitated the spread of er-
roneous opinions. Today it is a commonplace to la-
ment the death-roll on the roads caused by the advent
of the motor car; and even some scientists deplore
their own discovery of ways and means to release
atomic energy because of the catastrophic uses to
which it can be, and has been, put. Such objections
have not availed in the past, and seem unlikely to avail
in the future, to stay the advance of new discoveries

[8] For a fuller discussion, see the author's *The New Society* (London: Macmillan & Co.; 1951), Ch. 4 *passim*.

and inventions. What we have learned of the techniques and potentialities of mass propaganda cannot be simply obliterated. It is no more possible to return to the small-scale individualist democracy of Lockeian or liberal theory, partially realized in Great Britain in the middle years of the nineteenth century, than it is possible to return to the horse and buggy or to early *laissez-faire* capitalism. But the true answer is that these evils also carry with them their own corrective. The remedy lies not in a cult of irrationalism or a renunciation of the extended role of reason in modern society, but in a growing consciousness from below as well as from above of the role which reason can play. This is not a utopian dream at a time when the increasing use of reason at all levels of society is being forced on us by our technological and scientific revolution. Like every other great advance in history, this advance has its costs and its losses, which have to be paid, and its dangers, which have to be faced. Yet, in spite of sceptics, and cynics, and prophets of disaster, especially among the intellectuals of countries whose former privileged position has been undermined, I shall not be ashamed to treat it as a signal example of progress in history. It is perhaps the most striking and revolutionary phenomenon of our time.

The second aspect of the progressive revolution through which we are passing is the changed shape of the world. The great period of the fifteenth and sixteenth centuries, in which the mediaeval world finally broke up in ruins and the foundations of the modern world were laid, was marked by the discovery of new continents and by the passing of the world centre of gravity from the shores of the Mediterranean to those of the Atlantic. Even the lesser upheaval of the French revolution had its geographical sequel in the calling in of the new world to redress the balance of the old. But the changes wrought by the twentieth-century revolution are far more sweeping than anything that has happened since the sixteenth century. After some four hundred years the world centre of gravity has definitely shifted away from Western Europe. Western Europe, together with the outlying parts of the English-speaking world, has become an appanage of the North American continent, or, if you like, an agglomeration in which the United States serves both as power house and as control tower. Nor is this the only, or perhaps the most significant, change. It is by no means clear that the world centre of gravity now resides, or will continue for long to reside, in the English-speaking world, with its Western European annex. It appears to be the great land-mass of Eastern Europe and Asia, with its extensions into Africa, which today calls the tune in world affairs. The "unchanging East" is nowadays a singularly worn-out *cliché*.

Let us take a quick look at what has happened to Asia in the present century. The story begins with the Anglo-Japanese alliances of 1902—the first admission of an Asiatic country to the charmed circle of Euro-

pean Great Powers. It may perhaps be regarded as a
coincidence that Japan signalized her promotion by
challenging and defeating Russia, and, in so doing,
kindled the first spark which ignited the great twentieth-century revolution. The French revolutions of
1789 and 1848 had found their imitators in Europe.
The first Russian revolution of 1905 awakened no
echo in Europe, but found its imitators in Asia: in the
next few years revolutions occurred in Persia, in Tur-
key, and in China. The First World War was not
precisely a world war, but a European civil war—as-
suming such an entity as Europe existed—with world-
wide consequences: these included the stimulation of
industrial development in many Asian countries, of
anti-foreign feeling in China, and of Indian nationalism, and the birth of Arab nationalism. The Russian
revolution of 1917 provided a further and decisive
impulse. What was significant here was that its leaders
looked persistently, but in vain, for imitators in Europe, and finally found them in Asia. It was Europe
that had become "unchanging," Asia that was on the
move. I need not continue this familiar story down to
the present time. The historian is hardly yet in a position to assess the scope and significance of the Asian
and African revolutions. But the spread of modern
technological and industrial processes, and of the beginnings of education and political consciousness, to
millions of the population of Asia and Africa, is changing the face of those continents; and, while I cannot
peer into the future, I do not know of any standard

of judgment which would allow me to regard this as anything but a progressive development in the perspective of world history. The changed shape of the world resulting from these events has brought with it a relative decline in the weight, certainly of this country, perhaps of the English-speaking countries as a whole, in world affairs. But relative decline is not absolute decline; and what disturbs and alarms me is not the march of progress in Asia and Africa, but the tendency of dominant groups in this country—and perhaps elsewhere—to turn a blind or uncomprehending eye on these developments, to adopt towards them an attitude oscillating between mistrustful disdain and affable condescension, and to sink back into a paralysing nostalgia for the past.

What I have called the expansion of reason in our twentieth-century revolution has particular consequences for the historian; for the expansion of reason means, in essence, the emergence into history of groups and classes, of peoples and continents that hitherto lay outside it. In my first lecture I suggested that the tendency of mediaeval historians to view mediaeval society through the spectacles of religion was due to the exclusive character of their sources. I should like to pursue this explanation a little further. It has, I think, correctly, though no doubt with some exaggeration, been said that the Christian church was "the one rational institution of the Middle Ages." [9]

---

[9] Von Martin: *The Sociology of the Renaissance*, p. 18.

Being the one rational institution, it was the one historical institution; it alone was subject to a rational
course of development which could be comprehended
by the historian. Secular society was moulded and or-
ganized by the church, and had no rational life of its
own. The mass of people belonged, like pre-historic
peoples, to nature rather than to history. Modern history begins when more and more people emerge into
social and political consciousness, become aware of
their respective groups as historical entities having a
past and a future, and enter fully into history. It is
only within the last two hundred years at most, even
in a few advanced countries, that social, political, and
historical consciousness has begun to spread to anything like a majority of the population. It is only today
that it has become possible for the first time even to
imagine a whole world consisting of peoples who have
in the fullest sense entered into history and become
the concern, no longer of the colonial administrator
or of the anthropologist, but of the historian.

This is a revolution in our conception of history. In
the eighteenth century history was still a history of
élites. In the nineteenth century British historians began, haltingly and spasmodically, to advance towards
a view of history as the history of the whole national
community. J. R. Green, a rather pedestrian historian,
won fame by writing the first *History of the English
People*. In the twentieth century every historian pays
lip-service to this view; and, though performance lags
behind profession, I shall not dwell on these short-

comings, since I am much more concerned with our
failure as historians to take account of the widening
horizon of history outside this country and outside
Western Europe. Acton in his report of 1896 spoke of
universal history as "that which is distinct from the
combined history of all countries." He continued:

> It moves in a succession to which the nations are sub-
> sidiary. Their story will be told, not for their own sake,
> but in reference and subordination to a higher series, ac-
> cording to the time and degree in which they contribute
> to the common fortunes of mankind.[1]

It went without saying for Acton that universal history, as he conceived it, was the concern of any serious
historian. What are we at present doing to facilitate
the approach to universal history in this sense?

I did not intend in these lectures to touch on the
study of history in this university: but it provides me
with such striking examples of what I am trying to
say that it would be cowardly of me to avoid grasping
the nettle. In the past forty years we have made a
substantial place in our curriculum for the history of
the United States. This is an important advance. But
it has carried with it a certain risk of reinforcing the
parochialism of English history, which already weighs
like a dead hand on our curriculum, with a more in-
sidious and equally dangerous parochialism of the

---

[1] *The Cambridge Modern History: Its Origin, Authorship and
Production*, p. 14.

English-speaking world. The history of the English-
speaking world in the last four hundred years has
beyond question been a great period of history. But
to treat it as the centre-piece of universal history, and
everything else as peripheral to it, is an unhappy dis-
tortion of perspective. It is the duty of a university to
correct such popular distortions. The school of modern
history in this university seems to me to fall short in
the discharge of this duty. It is surely wrong that a
candidate should be allowed to sit for an honours degree in history in a major university without an adequate knowledge of any modern language other than
English; let us take warning by what happened in
Oxford to the ancient and respected discipline of philosophy when its practitioners came to the conclusion
that they could get on very nicely with plain everyday
English. It is surely wrong that no facilities should be
offered to the candidate to study the modern history
of any continental European country above the text-
book level. A candidate possessing some knowledge of
the affairs of Asia, Africa, or Latin America has at
present a very limited opportunity of displaying it in a
paper called, with magnificent nineteenth-century
panache, "The Expansion of Europe." The title unfortunately fits the contents: the candidate is not invited to know anything even of countries with an important and well-documented history like China or
Persia except what happened when the Europeans
attempted to take them over. Lectures are, I am told,
delivered in this university on the history of Russia

and Persia and China—but not by members of the faculty of history. The conviction expressed by the professor of Chinese in his inaugural lecture five years ago that "China cannot be regarded as outside the mainstream of human history" [2] has fallen on deaf ears among Cambridge historians. What may well be regarded in the future as the greatest historical work produced in Cambridge during the past decade has been written entirely outside the history department, and without any assistance from it: I refer to Dr. Needham's *Science and Civilization in China.* This is a sobering thought. I should not have exposed these domestic sores to the public gaze but for the fact that I believe them to be typical of most other British universities and of British intellectuals in general in the middle years of the twentieth century. That stale old quip about Victorian insularity, "Storms in the Channel—the Continent Isolated," has an uncomfortably topical ring today. Once more storms are raging in the world beyond; and, while we in the English-speaking countries huddle together and tell ourselves in plain everyday English that other countries and other continents are isolated by their extraordinary behaviour from the boons and blessings of our civilization, it sometimes looks as if we, by our inability or unwillingness to understand, were isolating ourselves from what is really going on in the world.

· · ·

---

[2] Edwin George Pulleyblank: *Chinese History and World History* (Cambridge University Press; 1955), p. 36.

In the opening sentences of my first lecture I drew attention to the sharp difference of outlook which separates the middle years of the twentieth century from the last years of the nineteenth. I should like in conclusion to develop this contrast; and, if in this context I use the words "liberal" and "conservative," it will be readily understood that I am not using them in their sense as labels for British political parties. When Acton spoke of progress, he did not think in terms of the popular British concept of "gradualism." "The Revolution, or as we say Liberalism," is a striking phrase from a letter of 1887. "The method of modern progress," he said in a lecture on modern history ten years later, "was revolution"; and in another lecture he spoke of "the advent of general ideas which we call revolution." This is explained in one of his unpublished manuscript notes: "The Whig governed by compromise: the Liberal begins the reign of ideas." [3] Acton believed that "the reign of ideas" meant liberalism, and that liberalism meant revolution. In Acton's

---

[3] For these passages see Acton: *Selections from Correspondence* (London: Longmans, Green & Co.; 1917), p. 278; *Lectures on Modern History*, pp. 4, 32; Add. MSS. 4949 (in Cambridge University Library). In the letter of 1887 quoted above, Acton marks the change from the "old" to the "new" Whigs (*i.e.* the Liberals) as "the discovery of conscience": "conscience" here is evidently associated with the development of "consciousness" (see pp. 179–80 above), and corresponds to "the reign of ideas." Stubbs also divided modern history into two periods separated by the French revolution: "the first a history of powers, forces, and dynasties; the second, a history in which ideas take the place of both rights and forms" (W. Stubbs: *Seventeen Lectures on the Study of Mediaeval and Modern History*, 3rd. ed. [1900], p. 239).

lifetime, liberalism had not yet spent its force as a dynamic of social change. In our day, what survives of liberalism has everywhere become a conservative factor in society. It would be meaningless today to preach a return to Acton. But the historian is concerned, first to establish where Acton stood, secondly to contrast his position with that of contemporary thinkers, and thirdly to enquire what elements in his position may be still valid today. The generation of Acton suffered, no doubt, from overweening self-confidence and optimism, and did not sufficiently realize the precarious nature of the structure on which its faith rested. But it possessed two things of both of which we are badly in need today: a sense of change as a progressive factor in history, and belief in reason as our guide for the understanding of its complexities.

Let us now listen to some voices of the 1950's. I quoted in an earlier lecture Sir Lewis Namier's expression of satisfaction that, while "practical solutions" were sought for "concrete problems," "programmes and ideals are forgotten by both parties," and his description of this as a symptom of "national maturity." [4] I am not fond of these analogies between the life-span of individuals and that of nations; and, if such an analogy is invoked, it tempts one to ask what follows when we have passed the stage of "maturity." But what interests me is the sharp contrast drawn between the practical and the concrete, which are praised, and

---

[4] See p. 47 above.

"programmes and ideals," which are condemned. This exaltation of practical action over idealistic theorizing is, of course, the hall-mark of conservatism. In Namier's thought it represents the voice of the eighteenth century, of England at the accession of George III, protesting against the impending onset of Acton's revolution and reign of ideas. But the same familiar expression of out-and-out conservatism in the form of out-and-out empiricism is highly popular in our day. It may be found in its most popular form in Professor Trevor-Roper's remark that, "when radicals scream that victory is indubitably theirs, sensible conservatives knock them on the nose." [5] Professor Oakeshott offers us a more sophisticated version of this fashionable empiricism: in our political concerns, he tells us, we "sail a boundless and bottomless sea," where there is "neither starting-point nor appointed destination," and where our sole aim can be "to keep afloat on an even keel."[6] I need not pursue the catalogue of recent writers who have denounced political "utopianism" and "messianism"; these have become the current terms of opprobrium for far-reaching radical ideas on the future of society. Nor shall I attempt to discuss recent trends in the United States, where historians and political theorists have had less inhibitions than their colleagues in this country in openly proclaiming their allegiance to conservatism. I will quote only a re-

---

[5] *Encounter*, Vol. VII, No. 6 (June 1957), p. 17.
[6] Oakeshott: *Political Education* (Cambridge University Press; 1951), p. 22.

mark by one of the most distinguished and most moderate of American conservative historians, Professor Samuel Morison of Harvard, who in his presidential address to the American Historical Association in December 1950 thought that the time had come for a reaction against what he called "the Jefferson-Jackson-F. D. Roosevelt line" and pleaded for a history of the United States "written from a sanely conservative point of view." [7]

But it is Professor Popper who, at any rate in Great Britain, has once more expressed this cautious conservative outlook in its clearest and most uncompromising form. Echoing Namier's rejection of "programmes and ideals," he attacks policies which allegedly aim at "re-modelling the 'whole of society' in accordance with a definite plan," commends what he calls "piecemeal social engineering," and does not apparently shrink from the imputation of "piecemeal tinkering" and "muddling through." [8] On one point, indeed, I should pay tribute to Professor Popper. He remains a stout defender of reason, and will have no truck with past or present excursions into irrationalism. But, if we look into his prescription of "piecemeal social engineering," we shall see how limited is the role which he assigns to reason. Though his definition of "piecemeal engineering" is not very precise, we are

[7] *American Historical Review*, Vol. LVI, No. 2 (January 1951), pp. 272–3.

[8] K. Popper, *The Poverty of Historicism* (London: Routledge & Kegan Paul; 1957), pp. 67, 74.

specifically told that criticism of "ends" is excluded; and the cautious examples which he gives of its legitimate activities—"constitutional reform" and "a tendency towards a greater equalization of incomes"—show plainly that it is intended to operate within the assumptions of our existing society.[9] The status of reason in Professor Popper's scheme of things is, in fact, rather like that of a British civil servant, qualified to administer the policies of the government in power and even to suggest practical improvements to make them work better, but not to question their fundamental presuppositions or ultimate purposes. This is useful work: I, too, have been a civil servant in my day. But this subordination of reason to the assumptions of the existing order seems to me in the long run wholly unacceptable. This is not how Acton thought of reason when he propounded his equation: revolution—liberalism—the reign of ideas. Progress in human affairs, whether in science or in history or in society, has come mainly through the bold readiness of human beings not to confine themselves to seeking piecemeal improvements in the way things are done, but to present fundamental challenges in the name of reason to the current way of doing things and to the avowed or hidden assumptions on which it rests. I look forward to a time when the historians and sociologists and political thinkers of the English-speaking world will regain their courage for that task.

---

[9] Ibid., pp. 64, 68.

It is, however, not the waning of faith in reason among the intellectuals and the political thinkers of the English-speaking world which perturbs me most, but the loss of the pervading sense of a world in perpetual motion. This seems at first sight paradoxical; for rarely has so much superficial talk been heard of changes going on around us. But the significant thing is that change is no longer thought of as achievement, as opportunity, as progress, but as an object of fear. When our political and economic pundits prescribe, they have nothing to offer us but the warning to mistrust radical and far-reaching ideas, to shun anything that savours of revolution, and to advance—if advance we must—as slowly and cautiously as we can. At a moment when the world is changing its shape more rapidly and more radically than at any time in the last four hundred years, this seems to me a singular blindness, which gives ground for apprehension, not that the world-wide movement will be stayed, but that this country—and perhaps other English-speaking countries—may lag behind the general advance, and relapse helplessly and uncomplainingly into some nostalgic backwater. For myself I remain an optimist; and when Sir Lewis Namier warns me to eschew programmes and ideals, and Professor Oakeshott tells me that we are going nowhere in particular and that all that matters is to see that nobody rocks the boat, and Professor Popper wants to keep that dear old T-model on the road by dint of a little piecemeal engineering, and Professor Trevor-Roper knocks screaming radicals on the nose, and Professor Morison pleads for history written in a sane conservative spirit, I shall look out on a world in tumult and a world in travail, and shall answer in the well-worn words of a great scientist: "And yet—it moves."

INDEX

A NOTE ON THE TYPE

THE TEXT of this book is set in ELECTRA, a Linotype face designed by W. A. Dwiggins (1880–1956). This face cannot be classified as either modern or old-style. It is not based on any historical model, nor does it echo any particular period or style. It avoids the extreme contrasts between thick and thin elements that mark most modern faces, and attempts to give a feeling of fluidity, power, and speed.

Composed by Kingsport Press, Inc.,
Kingsport, Tennessee.
Printed and bound by The Haddon Craftsmen, Inc.,
Scranton, Pennsylvania
Typography and binding design based on
originals by
W . A . D W I G G I N S